Advance Praise for /

This amazing book is loaded with lessons and important ideas! Read it, apply it, and let it change your life.

--Brian Tracy, Author/Speaker/Consultant

Master of Persuasion makes the step-by-step what to do easy. We don't have to be psychologists and invest years into learning how to do this. Do you have a Saturday morning? If so, read this book instead of eating donuts and watching cartoons. This book can change your life immediately. Make friends, build rapport, close, and sell in the most enjoyable way possible. If you don't have a free Saturday morning? Then read a chapter a day. It is easy to get hooked on what works.

—Tom "Big Al" Schreiter, Network Marketing Expert, International Speaker, and Best-Selling Author

This book helps you figure out how to be on the lookout for different types of body language when discussing things with others. As a parent I plan on using this information to help me connect more fully with my children, and as a business owner I plan on utilizing the information from this book to increase overall revenue.

—Andrea Carbine

What did I like/learn about *Master of Persuasion*? That I need to solve problems for other people before I can win big. I can see in my life and the lives of others that we have tried to get others to say YES for the wrong reasons. Persuading people is more effective than manipulating people. Let them make the Yes/No decision; they will be happier, as will I. Allowing people to say NO is okay, and life will still go on.

—Alan Gibson

Eric has a way of presenting a challenging concept and providing step-by-step instructions to not only understand it, but to succeed at it! Sales has always been a double-edged sword for me, in that I don't like it, but I need it in my business. I now have a win-win system for becoming a Master of Persuasion.

—Renee Renick, RN, Energy Psychology Mentor

This interactive book is jam-packed with actionable and useful exercises and information. It is presented in an organized manner to help you learn the art of persuasion and become a Master of Persuasion. Do the work, don't just read it. You will be amazed at the results!

—H. Braunius

We finished reading *Master of Persuasion* last night. As I read through it, I found myself realizing that many of the cues for effectively communicating work in all aspects of life. This book is not only a must-read but a must-study and put into action immediately. Thank you for the simple but effective techniques.

—Troy Anderson

Master of Persuasion is an inspirational, easy, and active read that is a great book not only for people in sales but for anyone who is striving for success in business and in life. I find the book to be a spiritual read because it promotes positive vibes, honesty, and virtues. I will go back and read this book over again when I am faced with challenges at work or in business.

—Maja Pcelica

Master of Persuasion has given me much to think about in terms of steps I can take (that are fully within my control) to maximize interactions with others so all sides feel like the interaction was a win-win scenario, which in turn increases the probability of many more such interactions in the future.

—Katherine Bess

This book feels like it was written just for me. I couldn't have read this book at a more perfect time. I can't wait to use the tools given in this book. I'm excited to see what will happen with my business after implementing everything I've learned.

—Andria Morgart

Master of
Persuasion

HOW TO DRAMATICALLY INCREASE SALES, GET PEOPLE TO SAY YES, AND BE A POSITIVE INFLUENCE IN THE LIVES OF OTHERS

ERIC BAILEY

DEDICATION

This book is dedicated to the amazing mentors I have had in my life, especially my wife, Heather. Without all of you and the things you have taught me, none of this would have been possible. From the bottom of my heart, thank you!

Table of Contents

CHAPTER 1

THE ART OF PERSUASION

If you were asked who made the biggest impact on your life, how would you respond?

Would you like to be a major positive influence in the lives of others?

Are you a parent or future parent?

Are you a mentor, coach, network marketer, sales professional, teacher, or religious leader?

Would it be OK if you dramatically increased the resources you could use to make a difference in the world?

If you answered yes to any of the questions above, you are reading the right book.

The world desperately needs people who are capable, intelligent, and willing to stand up and make a difference. The fact that you are reading this book is evidence that you are one of them!

I took a major leap of faith in 2010.

I was making very little money working a job I couldn't stand. Simply waking each morning was drudgery because it meant I had to face yet another day. Deep down, I felt I was destined for greatness, yet as hard as I looked, nothing in my life seemed to be leading me down the path that would allow me to realize my full potential.

I was desperate for an opportunity—any opportunity, really—to do something greater with my life. Do you ever feel that way?

I jumped at the first opportunity that came my way.

Having struggled for many years with chronic shoulder pain, I was introduced to a supplement designed to alkalize the body. After taking the supplement for thirty days, to my surprise, my shoulder pain was gone. I learned that the company that made it was a network marketing company (a concept that, up to that point, was foreign to me), and that anyone who chose to share the supplements with others could receive commission checks and earn an excellent living.

I was hooked.

An opportunity presented itself, and I took it. I had visions of grandeur of hitting the ground running, having a huge line of people waiting to purchase these supplements from me and pay me real money from the moment I got started, which is exactly what happened ...

... with the exception of everything after getting started.

I quit my job, which meant I had no income coming in. As much time and effort as I put into my new business venture, I lacked the skills necessary for success.

The dreadful day eventually came when I had to approach my wife and say, "I am so sorry, my love. I didn't even make enough money to put food on the table for you or keep a roof over our heads this month."

My wife was expecting our second child at the time.

When a man, who is expected to be the protector and provider for his family, has to tell the woman he loves that he is unable to provide basic necessities for her, it forces him to make a choice: either give up and go back to the drawing board or figure out a way to turn things around for the better.

I know what it is like to be homeless. I know what it is like to be on the verge of losing everything.

I also know that certain skills, once mastered, can lead you to achieving the life you've always desired.

Certain skills can make the difference between an ordinary life and an extraordinary life, a life of mediocrity and a life of fulfillment. Certain skills, once mastered, took me from being entrenched in depression and addiction, on the verge of divorce, eighty pounds overweight, on welfare and homeless, and con- templating suicide to total freedom, a red-hot marriage with five beautiful children, releasing eighty pounds and getting in the best shape of my life, becoming a millionaire by age 30, and a life of total passion and fulfillment.

Put plainly, mastering certain skills made all the difference for me, and it can make all the difference for you as well.

Those skills all have to do with *persuasion*.

Persuasion, or the act of influencing someone from one way of thinking to another, is all around us. We are constantly in a state of persuading or being persuaded. It is those who *do* the persuading that usually have the most success in life.

Consider that for a moment.

Can you enter into and remain in a loving, committed relationship without persuading someone to take a chance and go out with you?

Can you successfully ask your boss for a raise without persuading him/her to give you one?

Can you expect your children to be obedient, respectful, and complete their homework and household chores without persuading them to do so?

Can you have a successful business without persuading others to invest in your products or services?

Of course not!

The sad truth is that the vast majority of businesses fail within their first few years of opening, most people will never achieve true financial freedom, most marriages end in divorce, most people in the United States are overweight, and most people settle for simply being "comfortable." Most people never achieve more than mediocrity because they fail to acquire the skills necessary to succeed.

Consider that as well.

How many more lonely men and women would find love and companionship if they mastered the art of persuading their love interests to take a chance on them?

How many more lives would be forever improved if network marketing professionals, who have life-changing products, mastered the art of persuading others to give their products a try?

How many trillions of dollars would be saved every year in obesity-related medical costs if more people mastered the art of persuading themselves to stay motivated to improve their health?

It is my intention with this book to arm you with the skills needed to create the life you desire and deserve. As you implement and practice these skills, you will notice your relationships improving, your income skyrocketing, your body becoming leaner (self-persuasion is a must!), and your everyday life seeming less stressful and more fulfilling. You will literally become unstoppable as you become a *Master of Persuasion!*

To help you get the most out of this book, I invite you to keep a *persuasion journal.* You will be doing several exercises in this journal throughout this book. Please do *not* read this book passively. Doing so would be an enormous disservice to yourself and to those whom you are here to serve.

You will notice the main focus of this book is helping you serve as many people as possible. Persuasion is all about serving others. Throughout this book, I may refer to these people as "potential buyers," "prospective clients," and the like, using such terms interchangeably. Even if you are not currently involved in direct selling or business, I use these terms to refer to those you are here to serve.

You will also notice the use of several forms of *suggestology,* which are strategies employed to keep your mind engaged so you can experience the highest level of transformation. I write my books the same way I teach my live seminars, meaning *you* are the star. As such, I may ask you to do seemingly odd things, such as placing your hand over your heart and making declarations out loud. If these bother you, you may skip them, but I strongly encourage you to do them. Persuasion, after all, begins with yourself. If you are unwilling to persuade yourself to do small and simple tasks, how can you expect to persuade others to get behind large and life-altering causes? Please do *not* read this book passively.

Take a moment, right now, and answer the following questions in your persuasion journal:

Persuasion is …

Persuasion skills are needed in the following areas …

It is important for me to learn to be more persuasive because …

How many answers did you come up with?

The information you are about to read literally transformed my life and the lives of people around the world. When you master the art of persuasion, you become an instrument of positive transformation in the lives of others. (Isn't that amazing!?!)

In this book, you will learn the most effective ways to influence others to make positive changes in their lives.

You will learn how to increase your personal value and help others do the same.

You will learn efficient ways to persuade others to consider your ideas and take appropriate action.

You will learn time-tested skills to build rapport and trust (the importance of which will be discussed later).

If you have life-changing products, services, or messages you would like to share with more people, you will learn how to effectively do so (and how to earn millions of dollars while you are at it).

You will learn the correct way to make sales in extremely enjoy-able ways, even if you currently believe yourself to be terrible at sales. (Sadly, a lot of people view selling negatively. They go in for job interviews, and the very first thing they ask is if the position involves sales. If it does, they run!)

You will learn how we took our closing ratio from less than 20% to over 90% in one-on-one or one-on-two sales (something that is nearly unheard of in any industry), selling products that range from $15.00 audio trainings to $75,000.00 mentoring packages.

In this book, you will learn the science behind why people say my absolute favorite word: YES!

If you understand the science of why people say yes, it is also important to understand the science of why people say no. Most amateur persuaders give in to what we call *objections*. Once you've learned and mastered the skills in this book, you will never have to overcome another ridiculous objection (e.g., "I need to think about it.") again. Ever. (I make mentoring offers for tens of thousands of dollars. Keep in mind that these offers are to "normal" people, not multi-millionaires, who are just beginning their journey to success, in most cases.)

You will learn how to read body language in this book. All bodies give off messages. This is evident in the fact that everyone has a *buying strategy* (more on that in Chapter 5). You can literally talk a person into or talk a person out of buying something that they were already sold on by the wording you use. Everyone gives away their specific buying strategy in their body language. If you don't know what the four buying strategies are or how to elicit them from potential buyers, you can dissuade someone from doing business with you. When you use the wrong words as you present your products or services to others, you can create a lose-lose situation for all involved: you lose out on potential revenue, and the potential buyer loses out on the life-changing product or service you could have provided had you known how to read body language, elicit their buying strategy, and adjust the words you used accordingly. You will learn how to do exactly that in this book.

You will learn how to increase your confidence and self-worth in this book.

Put plainly, this book can completely transform your life if you implement the strategies found within it.

You will probably be stretching far outside your comfort zone as you perform the exercises and implement the strategies you read. You may find yourself feeling triggered or tempted to skip some or all of the exercises. I invite you to be hyperaware of how you feel as you read this book. If you find yourself thinking any of the following phrases:

"I already know this."

"This is stupid."

"This will never work."

"I don't see the point of this."

"I'll just put this down for a while and start reading it again some other time."

"I'm not sure I agree with this."

"This is too scary."

"I'll do this later."

"I'm just going to read through this the first time. I'll do the exercises next time."

… or anything of the sort, I invite you to stop for a moment, take a deep breath in, blow it out slowly through your mouth, and recognize your subconscious mind's pattern of playing tricks on you.

Your subconscious mind is designed to keep you *alive*. Any time its natural programming feels threatened, it puts up walls in an attempt to "protect" you. Unfortunately, this "protection" usually keeps you from *thriving*. Growth and progress cannot happen within your comfort zone.

There are two types of people in the world: *dabblers* and *finishers*. Dabblers often have fantastic ideas and big dreams. Sadly, they almost never stick with any one idea or dream until it becomes successful.

I invite you to be a *finisher. Finishers* are *married* to their ideas and dreams; they stay committed until the very end. Stick with this book until you finish it, complete all the exercises within it, and implement its strategies in your everyday life. Avoid the temptation to simply *learn* persuasion skills. Instead, allow yourself to *become* a master of persuasion. If, by doing so, you positively change just one person's life, won't it all be worth it? How much more valuable will you be when you're able to help transform the lives of many people?

Write the following commitment in your persuasion journal:

I am a finisher. I finish every positive project I start. I commit to finishing this book, completing all exercises, and implementing all strategies to become a master of persuasion.

Now place your hand over your heart and declare, "I am a master of persuasion!"

Begin

Persuasion begins in the first ten seconds of meeting someone. A first impression can determine whether or not someone will like you, pay attention to you, trust you, or buy from you.

Have you ever met someone and simply felt "off" from the moment that person approached you?

Have you ever experienced someone approaching you and giving you the feeling that they only cared about selling you something?

Audience members do an interesting exercise the first day of our live Master of Persuasion seminar, during which they spend a number of minutes going around the room meeting people under different scenarios while paying attention to what they see in others and how they feel.

The first exercise involves pretending that everyone else in the room is a complete waste of space and imagining they would rather be anywhere else in the world except there at the class. When asked about the experience, audience members report that others exhibit little to no eye contact and seem distant and closed off. They report feeling weak, sad, disappointed, and wanting to hide.

Your thoughts and intentions have a physiological effect on your body and the bodies of those around you. You can literally influence the health and well-being of others by the thoughts you think.

Do you know families that seem to always have at least one member of the household that is sick? Is it possible there could be some "stinkin' thinkin'" taking place in that household, including poor attitudes, victim mentalities, and unhappy demeanors?

Do you know people who always seem to look on the bright side of life? That exhibit a passion for life and always have a positive word to say? Are they usually healthy and happy? How do you feel when you are around them? Do you notice yourself feeling bright, cheerful, and energized in their presence?

Write the following in your persuasion journal:

My thoughts and intentions have a physiological effect on my body and the bodies of those around me. I choose to have a positive attitude in everything I do.

Now place your hand over your heart and declare, "I am a master of persuasion!"

Next, audience members imagine they've just quit their jobs to sign up to be distributors for a network marketing company and, as the sole provider for their household with no other source of income, desperately need to enroll as many other people as possible into their network marketing company.

Can you imagine what that scene looks like?

While the energy is significantly higher, happier, and friendlier than the first exercise, audience members report feeling hollow and inauthentic. They feel that others don't genuinely care about them but only want to sell them something and get their money.

A number of years ago, I had the crazy idea that the moment I left my full-time job and opened my own business I would have an enormous line of people waiting to pay me money and receive my services. Because I didn't have any income coming in to provide for my family, I viewed every person who came into my office as a walking dollar sign.

How do you think that made them feel?

Instead of leaving my office feeling calmer, more peaceful, and happier, they left with an unsettled feeling because they picked up on my intention to get as much money as possible from their wallets into my own.

Back to our live events: I then invite audience members to meet as many people as possible while thinking, "I love you and genuinely want to serve you."

The difference in the energy between this and the other two exercises is astounding.

Audience members report feeling connected, more engaged, authentic, and happier. Their body language is more relaxed, open, and inviting. There are tears of joy and many hugs given and received during the two minutes they perform this exercise.

Once a mentor pointed out the power our thoughts and intentions have in influencing others, I made a conscious effort to shift my thoughts from "How can I get as much of your money as possible?" to "How may I best serve and support you?" As I interacted with my clients, I thought, "You are amazing! Thank you for allowing me to serve you!"

Can you guess what happened?

My closing ratio increased from 25% to over 90%. My existing clientele referred several more people and started asking what other services I offered. My income tripled from one month to the next and continued to increase dramatically throughout the following year.

Money comes from other people. People will give you money when you provide a product or service that solves a problem, fills a need, or satisfies a desire in their life. When you focus on making *money*, you push people away. When you focus on loving, serving, and supporting *people,* you end up with much more money.

Write the following in your persuasion journal:

Instead of focusing on making money, I focus on loving, serving, and supporting more people. The greater number of people whose problems I solve, needs I fill, and desires I help satisfy, the more money I will earn.

Now place your hand over your heart and declare, "I am a master of persuasion!"

The first impressions you create help build or break *rapport.* Rapport is the level of responsiveness between people. When you build high levels of rapport with someone, he or she will usually respond extremely positively to your ideas and suggestions. When you break rapport, he or she usually will not.

"So how do I build rapport with people, Eric?"

Most people tend to like and respond more positively with people who are like them or like those they desire to become. When you pay attention to subtle movements, language, body language, tone, and gestures the people with whom you interact make and then use similar movements, language, body language, tone, and gestures, you can begin to build rapport.

Consider the following examples:

How do you tend to greet people you meet for the first time? Do you keep your distance? Do you offer a hug? Do you extend a hand for the person to shake? When you shake someone's hand, do you try to be as firm as possible? Do you offer what I call the "limp fish" handshake (use your imagination!)? How do you feel when someone extends the same greeting in return?

How much eye contact do you usually like to give? When others speak to you, do you like to look them directly in the eyes or look somewhere else (such as their nose, mouth, or hands)? How long do you like to maintain eye contact before you look away? How does it feel when someone matches your level of eye contact?

Do you tend to be a rapid speaker or a slow speaker? What kind of words do you use to describe things? Do you use slang? Are there certain terms that only someone who grew up in your hometown would know and use? How do you feel when you meet someone for the first time who speaks at the same pace as you and uses the slang from your hometown or area?

What kind of gestures do you use? Do you tend to be more ani-mated when speaking or more reserved? How do you feel when you meet someone who uses gestures like you do?

A simple way to build rapport is *matching and mirroring.* This means paying attention to the subtle things (like the ones mentioned above) those with whom you interact do and then matching them. Of course, you would not want to be obvious in your approach, nor would you want to do so in a mocking manner. This does *not* mean each time the person you're with scratches his nose, you scratch your nose, or each time she crosses her legs, you cross your legs. It simply means finding ways to match a few of their gestures, such as recip-rocating the initial greeting they give you, speaking at a similar pace, and using the same language they use to describe things. (This last one is especially important in sales. If your potential buyer tells you they are looking for a "beautiful home," and you tell them you have a "very pretty home" to show them, this can break rapport. In your mind, "beautiful" and "very pretty" may mean the same thing, but it probably won't to them. Always pay attention to the language they use and repeat it, word for word, when appropriate. We'll discuss this more in Chapter 5.)

Sadly, we live in a society where most people *break* rapport before they ever build it.

Have you ever tried to share something you were extremely passionate about with someone, only to find them staring at their phone throughout the entire conversation or otherwise not reciprocating your level of excitement? How did that make you feel? Did it increase or decrease your desire to share exciting news with them in the future? In most cases, this would decrease one's desire to share exciting news because it would break rapport.

Is this making sense?

Write the following in your persuasion journal:

Rapport is power. I can build rapport by appropriately matching and mirroring those with whom I interact. Building rapport increases the likelihood that people will respond positively to my ideas, suggestions, products, and services.

Now place your hand over your heart and declare, "I am a master of persuasion!"

Want to take rapport to yet another level?

As you've already learned, our thoughts and intentions can positively or negatively affect the physiology of those around us. People are naturally drawn toward people and things that help them feel good. When you send people compliments in your mind, you literally improve the physical, mental, and emotional state of those around you.

I demonstrate this principle at my live Master of Persuasion events by inviting a volunteer to join me on stage and extend his or her non dominant arm at a ninety-degree angle away from their body. I inform them that I will apply downward pressure to their arm with my hands and that they should resist me, meaning not allow me to push their arm down to their side. Most of the time, they can do so extremely easily. I invite the audience to think compliments in their minds about the person on stage, such as, "You are beautiful," "You are amazing," "You are capable," "You are enough." While they do so, I apply significantly more pressure to the volunteer's arm. In most cases, I cannot push their arm down regardless of how much pressure I apply to it or how hard I push.

I then invite the audience to think such thoughts as, "You are ugly," "You are worthless," "You can't do it," or "Give me all your money." Can you guess what happens? I am able to push the volunteer's arm down with very little pressure.

When you think positive thoughts about the people with whom you interact, it causes them to feel a little better at a subconscious level. This links interacting with you with feeling good.

Again, most people tend to be drawn to people and things that help them feel good, so it becomes much more likely that they will want to continue to be around you. This is especially effective during physical interactions, such as an initial handshake. During the brief moment you shake someone's hand, think, "You are amazing!" Watch closely. You may just see them smile a little more as they subconsciously receive your compliment.

This can also be done remotely.

The energy from your thoughts and intentions has no boundaries. Is there someone whom you need to reach who never answers their phone when you call? As you dial his or her number, think such thoughts as, "I love you! You are amazing! I would love to serve and support you! Thank you for accepting my call and answering your phone!" The other person will subconsciously pick up on something that is helping them to feel good and will be more drawn to whatever is causing that feeling (in this case, you on the other end of the phone).

"So, Eric, does that mean this will work every single time? Like 100% of the people I call will magically answer every time I send them compliments?"

No, but it significantly increases the odds that they will respond.

If you are in sales, what kind of difference would, say, a ten percent increase in responsiveness from your potential buyers make in your level of income? What kind of difference would a twenty or thirty or fifty percent increase make? This "ninja skill" takes no extra time, so why not give it a try?

"Eric, that seems hokey! What evidence do you have that sending people compliments in their mind actually makes a difference?"

Besides the direct impact this has had on my income and the income of my clients who utilize this tool, I invite you to read *The Hidden Messages in Water* by Dr. Masaru Emoto. Dr. Emoto details the science behind the effect our thoughts and intentions have in water molecules. Don't scientists say our bodies are primarily made of water?

Write the following in your persuasion journal:

My thoughts and intentions have a physiological effect on those around me. I think positive thoughts about myself and about those with whom I interact.

Now place your hand over your heart and declare, "I am a master of persuasion!"

Master of Persuasion

CHAPTER 2

LESS PERSUASIVE vs. MASTERS OF PERSUASION

There are several differences between less persuasive people and masters of persuasion, some of which may seem counterintuitive or go against strategies you were taught in the past. This is because the art of persuasion has shifted dramatically over the last few decades, especially in the last few years. What used to work, particularly in regard to sales, simply doesn't work anymore. It is critical to stay ahead of the game when it comes to persuasion.

Less persuasive people keep bugging you until you give the answer they want. They persist, nag, and pound until they beat you into submission, never taking into account the answers you've already given them or what may be in your best interest. You may give them a few yeses to get them off the phone or out of your house, but these yeses are rarely genuine. Those that do tell them yes often back out of their commitment without actually following through.

Masters of persuasion are 100% OK hearing no. They genuinely have your best interest at heart, even if that means referring you to someone who may be a better fit for your individual needs. A gentleman recently came into one of my clinics to be treated for chronic shoulder pain. As effective as my practitioners are in what they do to eliminate shoulder pain, after treating him for a few minutes, I strongly felt that his body needed treatments my company does not provide.

"I need to apologize to you," I told him. "I'm afraid what I do isn't what your body needs at this time."

He gave me a weird look which implied, "Wait, aren't you going to try to talk me into signing up for a lengthy treatment plan with you?"

"As much as I would love to serve you further," I told him, "I want you to invest your hard-earned money into whatever treatment plan is going to give you the results you are looking for, and I do not feel what we do here is going to give that to you. There will be no charge for today's visit. Would it be OK if I referred you elsewhere?"

A look of gratitude spread across his face. He thanked me profusely for my time and for having his best interest at heart.

This does *not*, of course, mean you never want to practice persistence or get to the heart of why you hear "no" in the first place (we'll discuss this more in depth in Chapter 6). There have been several instances of prospective clients who told me "no" initially because they didn't have enough information to say "yes" or because they had a concern they had not yet expressed to me. After respectfully asking if I could learn the reason why they felt the way they did, I was able to ease their concern, give them the information needed, and turn their original "no" into a very committed "yes."

When you are 100% OK hearing "No," you avoid *desperate energy.*

Have you ever been approached by someone who seemed desperate for you to say "Yes"? How did they make you feel? Did you feel more inclined to say "Yes" or "No"?

Desperate energy causes most people to be more inclined to say "No." Being 100% OK with hearing "No" allows you to receive many more "Yeses."

Write the following in your persuasion journal:

I always have the best interest of others at heart. I am 100% OK hearing "No," even if that means referring potential clients elsewhere. Being 100% OK hearing "No" leads to me hearing "Yes" much more often.

Now place your hand over your heart and declare, "I am a master of persuasion!"

"That's all fine and dandy, Eric, but rejection is one of my biggest fears! How do I get to the point where I can honestly be OK hearing 'No'?"

Consider the following three tips:

1. Replace any thoughts about money with loving thoughts toward your potential client.

As we've already discussed, people pick up on our thoughts and intentions. If you think about the money you will make if a person says yes, this can turn the potential client off and turn what could have been a yes into a no. If any thought about money enters your mind (even for a split second), immediately replace it with loving thoughts about the prospect, such as, "You are amazing! You are incredible! I would love to serve and support you in any way I can! You are brilliant!" Keep your thoughts and intentions directed to serving the other person, even if that means referring them to someone else.

2. Make it a game.

No matter how high your closing ratio is, you're going to hear some "No's" on your way to hearing a "Yes." What kind of difference would it make if you absolutely *loved* receiving "No's" just as much as you loved hearing "Yes"? Set a goal for yourself each day to receive a certain number of "No's" and a reward when you reach this goal. Each "No" you receive takes you one step closer to getting your reward. Do the same thing with "Yeses." This turns a potentially "negative" situation (hearing "no") into a positive situation. It becomes a win-win for you regardless of how prospects respond to your offer.

3. Be mindful of your personal needs.

Persuasion isn't always easy. Rejection is part of the game. Make sure to take good care of yourself each day to avoid falling into *rejection depression*. Rejection depression can happen when someone experiences a long bout of "no's" without any "yeses." It causes them to think, "What's the point? I'm getting nowhere. Why bother trying anymore?" You can avoid rejection depression by utilizing the first two tips and by making sure your basic needs are always taken care of. Make sure you get a full night's sleep each night so you are fully rested, eat a healthy diet, exercise regularly, allow yourself "me time" each day to pursue positive hobbies, and take time to unwind every day. Rejection depression is the enemy of productivity. Taking time for yourself for passive self-nurturing keeps your head and your heart in the right place and helps you stay as productive as possible.

Less persuasive people often *pressure*, *coerce*, and *manipulate*. The biggest difference between *persuasion* and *manipulation* is *intention*. Persuasion means influencing someone into a win-win situation, meaning you both equally benefit. Manipulation means influencing someone into a win-lose situation, meaning the person being manipulated benefits much less (or not at all) than the person doing the manipulating.

There are many who believe all forms of sales have to do with manipulation, so they avoid selling at all costs. What they don't realize is that selling, in its purest form, involves *persuasion,* meaning inviting someone into a *win-win* situation, rather than *manipulation*, or creating a *win-lose* situation. This is why it is important to always keep your potential clients' best interest in mind. (We will explain how to do this more in depth in Chapter 5.)

Masters of persuasion *suggest*, *nudge*, *encourage* and *invite*. They seek to empower others and empower themselves.

Less persuasive people focus on making *money*.

20

Masters of persuasion focus on serving *people*. They understand that if they can serve someone, and it's in that person's greatest and highest good for them to do some sort of exchange, they do it. But they also understand it may benefit someone more to be served by someone else. I have literally walked away from 5-figure checks from people wanting to hire me as their personal mentor because I felt in my heart that I wasn't the best mentor for them.

With that said, this does *not* mean giving away your products and services for free. While doing so may be appropriate on a few, select occasions, it often benefits people *more* to invest in the products and services they receive. This is especially true in the self-mastery industry. If you are a professional mentor or coach, it may be tempting to offer your services to loved ones at no charge. Please avoid this temptation. While there may be exceptions, most people get more out of something when they have skin in the game. People who *pay* tend to *pay attention*.

With that in mind, less persuasive people *disempower* others. I've heard professional mentors say, "I know you can't afford my services, so I'm just going to give them to you for free."

They literally project their own limiting beliefs about money onto their loved ones and rob them of the chance to invest in themselves.

Masters of persuasion *empower* others. Instead of *impossibility thinking* (i.e., "I know you can't afford this ..." "I know you can't ..." "Because you are unable to ..."), they help others tap into their own resourcefulness.

Tony Robbins says, "It is never a matter of resources but a matter of resourcefulness."

Consider that for a moment.

If someone wants or needs something enough, there is *always* a way to get it.

If someone you loved and took care of was in a life-threatening accident and needed life-saving surgery (which probably wouldn't be cheap), even if you only earned minimum wage, would you tell the doctors at the hospital to pull the plug because you don't have the money to afford the surgery, or would you plead with the doctors to perform the surgery because you would find a way to make it work?

When people express a lack of *resources*, validate their concern and then invite them to be *resourceful*.

"I don't have a way to get to your house for the get-together."

"I totally understand. Who could you ask to give you a ride?"

"I'm too busy to exercise."

"I totally understand being busy. How could you create the time to exercise?"

"I don't have the money for that."

"I totally understand. How could you earn the money for it? Could you donate plasma? Could you have a yard sale?"

This, of course, starts with you. We tend to attract people into our lives that are like ourselves. If you give in to disempowering excuses, you will probably attract others who do the same. You must be willing to persuade *yourself* if you want to effectively persuade *others*.

The key to this is turning your *excuses* into reasons why you *will*. For example:

"I'm not going to exercise; I don't have the energy," becomes "I'm going to exercise so I can have more energy." "I'm not going to sign up for that coaching program; I don't have the money," becomes "I'm going to sign up for that coaching program so I can learn to earn more money."

Write the following in your persuasion journal:

It is never a matter of resources but a matter of resourcefulness. I turn my *excuses* into *reasons*. I empower others to be resourceful and invest in themselves to reach their highest potential.

Now place your hand over your heart and declare, "I am a master of persuasion!"

Less persuasive people are often people-pleasers. They play small and avoid ruffling feathers to "keep the peace" and make sure no one dislikes them.

Something I noticed during the many years I worked in the restaurant industry is that some adults have come to learn that, if they throw a big enough tantrum, the people-pleasers of the world will give them their way. I saw several managers bend over backwards to accommodate ridiculous complaints and demands that went completely against our restaurant's policies in an attempt to please those who weren't willing to be pleased.

I'm going to be bold enough to suggest that, if you aren't ruffling any feathers, you aren't playing big enough.

No matter how great a person you are, there will always be opposition. Think of the greatest men and women to ever walk the earth. Those that brought about the greatest changes in the world made enemies, were criticized, mocked, hated, and (in some cases) martyred. Can you imagine how different our world would be without people like Martin Luther King Jr., Mother Teresa, Jesus Christ, and so on?

Masters of persuasion live their purpose regardless of how many feathers they ruffle. Mother Teresa had a poem on her wall that said, "Give the world your best, and you may get hurt. Give the world your best anyway!"

It is my personal belief that each of us came here to influence a certain number of people for good. The only way we can actually grow our influence to where it needs to be is by being willing to ruffle feathers.

This includes holding others to their word, including yourself.

Integrity means doing what you say you'll do when you say you'll do it. One's true character becomes evident when they are held to their word.

When you give your word, keep it!

When you say you'll do something, do it!

When you say you'll arrive somewhere at a certain time, don't you dare arrive even a single minute late! Doing so would violate your integrity. Arrive at the time you say you will arrive.

Set reminders for yourself, if needed. Keep a detailed calendar. Demonstrate *radical integrity*.

"But, Eric, what if, for example, I'm on my way to an appointment and run into traffic? What do I do then?"

Plan ahead and give yourself enough of a buffer that you can keep your word, even in the case of traffic or other delays.

"But what do I do if I give my word and then remember I already gave my word to do something else at the same time?"

In the rare case that something like this happens, reach out to the person you gave your word to and *ask for permission* to renegotiate the commitment in a *win-win* way. Make sure to do this *well in advance*. For example, if you book appointments with two different people for Tuesday at 2 p.m., reach out to both of them and say, "I apologize. I just realized I double booked myself for Tuesday at 2 p.m. Would it be possible to meet at a different time or on a different day?" Notice the honor and respect in that message. It apologizes and admits fault and then asks for permission to move the commitment in a way that honors both parties and creates a win-win situation. If one of them says that Tuesday at 2 p.m. is the only time that works, find a way that creates a win-win situation.

Do *not* say, "Sorry, I just realized I am scheduled somewhere else. I'm not going to come in on Tuesday." Doing so fails to ask for permission, does *not* create a win-win situation, and demonstrates a lack of integrity.

If an emergency arises that puts you behind schedule with someone you gave your word to meet at a certain time, contact them as soon as possible and ask permission to still come in. "I apologize, I had a bit of an emergency come up. My GPS says I will arrive at 4:04 p.m. instead of 4:00. Is it still OK if I come in?" If they say no, honor and respect their decision. If they say yes, be sure to get there by 4:04 p.m.

Demonstrating *radical integrity* will set you apart from the rest of the world that seems to view integrity as something to demonstrate only when convenient. You will build much greater rapport and higher levels of respect when you show this level of respect for others.

Dare to be different. Dare to go against the status quo. Dare to hold people to their word. Dare to stand up for what you believe in. Dare to become your absolute best self. And dare to be a light to those who live in darkness.

Write the following in your persuasion journal:

Masters of persuasion demonstrate *radical integrity.* I always keep my word.

Now place your hand over your heart and declare, "I am a master of persuasion!"

Less persuasive people accept *smoke screens.* Smoke screens are bogus excuses that hide the true reason for "choosing out," or saying no to someone or something.

I sold chocolate bars door-to-door as a kid to raise money for school field trips. While many gladly supported me by purchasing chocolate bars, there were many who would decline, saying things like, "No, thanks, I don't have any money," or "No, thanks, I'm allergic to chocolate." While this may have been true in some cases, most of the time, these were nothing more than smoke screens. Some people may not have liked the school I attended, some may not have liked the clothes I was wearing, some may have been having a rough day, and some simply weren't interested in supporting someone else's kid. They made excuses to hide the real reason they didn't want to purchase chocolate in an attempt to save face.

Masters of persuasion recognize smoke screens for what they are and love their potential buyers enough to find out their genuine concerns. Only when you find out what is hiding behind the "smoke" can you help determine what is in their best interest (we will detail how to do this in Chapter 6).

Less persuasive people support *indecision*. Indecision is one of the biggest destroyers of success and progress. Napoleon Hill, author of *Think and Grow Rich,* said, "Unsuccessful people tend to be very slow to make up their mind and very quick to change it." They tend to use *procrastination phrases*, such as:

"I'll think about …"

"Maybe one day …"

"Someday I'll …"

"I'm not ready …"

"Not right now …"

"I'll get back to you …"

"Let me sleep on it …"

"I'll pray about it …"

If you are a church-attending Christian like I am, that last one may hit a nerve.

"Eric, are you encouraging people not to pray about things!?!"

Of course not. But how many people do you know that hide behind their spirituality as a procrastination tool?

Napoleon Hill continues, "Successful people tend to be quick to make up their mind and slow to change it."

Masters of persuasion understand that the greatest opportunities in life usually don't last very long. If they feel impressed to opt into something, they take immediate action and "choose in." If they feel impressed to "choose out" of something, they say, "No, thank you," and respectfully walk away. They encourage their prospective clients to do the same.

When you are 100% OK whether the potential buyer says yes or no, you can create a safe, no-pressure environment to determine what is in their best interest to do. If it is in their best interest to decline, encourage them to decline. If it is in their best interest to agree, encourage them to agree.

I tell my prospective clients before I ever make them any sort of offer that I do not work with people who use procrastination phrases because such people usually don't get good results with the programs I offer. My programs require consistent action and progress, and those that use procrastination phrases sit around thinking about whether or not to take action instead of simply taking action.

I tell prospective clients that it is 100% OK to tell me, "No, thank you," if what I offer is not a fit for them and to only move forward if what I offer would help them achieve the result they desire. I ask for a firm commitment that, if I give them details of one or more of my programs or services, they will *not* use any procrastination phrases but will tell me either, "No, thank you," or "Yes, sign me up." If they break their word and still insist that they cannot make a decision, I lovingly and respectfully inform them that what I do is not for them.

This does *not* mean pressuring people to make the decision *you* want them to make. It simply means helping people uncover what is in *their* best interest and following through accordingly.

I do *not* support indecision because, the longer it takes to make a decision, the more opposing forces (such as fear and doubt) can influence that decision.

Indecision drains one's energy. Each decision that remains unmade is like a window on a computer or smartphone that remains open. When too many windows are left open, the device begins to slow down. If you consistently feel drained of energy, one possible reason is you may have too many decisions that remain to be made. T. Harv Eker said, "Taking one action is worth one hundred years of thinking about it."

Encouraging people to make quick decisions may come across as manipulation to some. Keep in mind that manipulation is influencing someone into any situation other than a win-win situation. When you support indecision, you automatically create a lose-lose situation. When you have your prospects' best interest at heart, help them break through their fears and take action on what will most benefit them, you create a win-win situation.

Write the following in your persuasion journal:

I support quick decision-making. When presented with opportunities, I make the best decision for myself and my family quickly by either saying, "No, thank you," or "Yes, please," and taking immediate appropriate action. I love my prospects enough to help them make the right decision for themselves quickly, even if that means encouraging them to say no.

Now place your hand over your heart and declare, "I am a master of persuasion!"

Less persuasive people have to be right (no matter how wrong they might be).

Have you ever met someone like that?

They could be arguing about astrophysics with someone with a PhD in astrophysics even though they've never even touched a book on the subject, and still they will argue that they are right about their opinion on astrophysics.

One of my mentors once said, "You have two choices: you can either be *right*, or you can be *rich*."

Masters of persuasion respect the opinions of others. They don't always need to have the last word. They are 100% OK if not everyone agrees with them. They understand that they are here to serve a specific type of person, and not everyone is going to fit that description.

Less persuasive people think they already know everything. They would never read a book like this. Why would they? They think they already know all the information this book contains, even though they've never so much as picked it up.

Masters of persuasion are teachable, humble, and consistently seek to learn more. They tend to be very calm and collected when they speak, emanating a confident, quiet dignity.

Less persuasive people need others to agree with them. When someone expresses an opposing opinion, they tend to argue, insult, and attack.

Masters of persuasion, when presented with an opposing opinion that refuses to be changed, remain calm and simply say, "That's an interesting opinion." They know that they know what they know, regardless of how many other people know that they know.

In summary:

Less Persuasive People	Masters of Persuasion
Demand the answer they want to hear	Are 100% OK hearing no
Pressure, coerce, and manipulate	Suggest, nudge, invite, and encourage
Focus on money	Focus on serving the person
Disempower others	Empower others
Are people-pleasers	Live their purpose, even if it ruffles feathers
Break their commitments	Demonstrate radical integrity
Accept smoke screens	Love people enough to find the root of their concerns

Support indecision	Help people make the right decision for themselves quickly
Have to be right	Respect the opinions of others
Think they know everything	Are teachable, humble, and consistently seek to learn more
Need others to agree with them	Are confident knowing that they know what they know, even if others disagree or don't know that they know

Understanding these principles will help you hear my favorite word much more often than otherwise. That word, of course, is "YES!"

CHAPTER 3

GETTING PEOPLE TO SAY YES!

W hat would your life be like if, more often than not, those whom you invite to take action said yes?

The most successful people in life have mastered the art of persuading others to say yes!

Consider that for a moment.

If you want someone special to marry you, you will need to persuade that person to say yes!

If you want your boss to give you a substantial raise, you will need to persuade him or her to say yes!

If you want to do well in business, you will need to offer your product or service to many people and persuade many people to say yes!

As with every aspect of persuasion, there is a science behind it.

There are eight major reasons why people say yes. When you learn and master this science, success becomes very simple.

Eight major reasons why people say yes

1) Reciprocity

There is a chain of grocery stores in Utah that brilliantly understands this principle. They have excellent products that most other stores don't carry, but the majority of items on their shelves are significantly more expensive than the same items found in other stores. Yet their store is always full of customers.

What keeps people loyal to that grocery store when they might save significant amounts of money if they shopped somewhere else?

They offer small hors d'oeuvres to everyone who enters the store. Usually it isn't anything more than a small cracker with some dip on it, something that costs the store pennies to provide, but it is enough.

This small gesture is sufficient for all who shop there to feel more inclined to purchase their household needs at this store.

Have you ever eaten a small sample of food at a grocery store and then felt more inclined to purchase that item? Reciprocity basically means "I give you something, therefore you feel more inclined to give me something in return." Car dealerships often offer a bottle of water to potential buyers. When you offer something of value to your potential buyers, they will be more likely to reciprocate and give you something of value in return.

2) Social Proof

Have you ever noticed small signs in hotel room bathrooms that ask you to reuse your towels throughout your stay in order to help "conserve resources"?

Let's be honest: Are most hotels really concerned about saving the earth? Maybe, maybe not. Hotels are businesses, and part of business is striving to cut costs whenever possible. Studies have shown that when hotels simply ask, "Would you please reuse your towels," very few people actually do, especially at higher-end hotels. On the flip side, hotels that say something like, "65% of people that stay in this room reuse their towels at least once," see most of their guests reuse their towels.

Most people want to be included in the majority. They want to feel like they belong. When they believe the majority of other people do something, they are more inclined to do whatever the majority does.

Have you ever had to decide between two similar restaurants? Imagine you have a craving for Mexican food, and there are two Mexican restaurants on the same corner. When you drive by, you see that one of them is completely empty, and the other is completely full. Which restaurant would you feel more inclined to visit?

Most people would go to the full restaurant. Why? That is what most other people are doing, so that restaurant must be better than the empty one. It could be that the full restaurant serves food that pales in comparison to the empty one, but if several people are enjoying it, it "must" be good.

A number of years ago, sitcoms added laugh tracks that would play any time a character made a joke. When the audience watching at home heard laughter, they had the thought that the show "must" be funny. Ratings improved significantly.

Most businesses have websites that include testimonials from happy clients, including my own. When people see that clients who have invested in Feel Well, Live Well programs have achieved such progress as releasing sixty-seven pounds in only three months, growing their monthly income from $700 to over $100,000.00 in only four months, and going from the verge of divorce with their spouse to marital bliss after only a single mentoring appointment, it adds validity to what my company offers. This social proof helps potential clients feel more inclined to do business with us.

3) Commitment

My company strives to be extremely generous and give back to the community, when possible. It is not uncommon for us to offer complimentary treatments at our clinics and full-ride scholarships to our seminars when we feel certain people would benefit from them.

At the same time, we understand that those people's lives cannot be improved if they do not show up to the clinic or attend the seminars, so we ask for a firm commitment from those to whom we offer these gifts. It is not uncommon for us, after setting a complimentary appointment with someone, to say, "I'm sure I'm totally preaching to the choir with you, but any time we set aside time in our calendar, we always make sure it is set in stone. If we put you down for __ (date) at ___ (time), will you 100% for sure be there?" If they respond with any hesitancy, we do not schedule the appointment.

Why?

Again, we understand that people's lives cannot be improved if they do not show up. People are much more likely to follow through with something if they've made a commitment.

I may even go so far as to ask for some form of collateral from prospective clients. For example, when someone registers for one of my live events, whether at full price or with a scholarship, I get charged for their class materials. If they then "no-show" the event, I am out the cost of those materials, not to mention the revenue I could have collected from someone paying full price for their seat. This is why I often require a valid credit card number to reserve the seat of someone registering with a scholarship code and a written agreement and authorization to charge their card for the cost of the class materials if they no-show the event. This allows them to have "skin in the game" and helps ensure they will follow through with their agreed-upon commitment.

4) Liking

If you had to choose between two people you could purchase a product from, would you rather purchase from someone you can't stand or from someone you know, like, and trust?

Most people would rather do business with someone they like, which is why building rapport is so important.

Does this mean everyone will like you? Of course not. Masters of persuasion understand that it is impossible to please everyone, but they still make an effort to be courteous, friendly, and respectful.

5) Authority

Imagine attending a fitness conference put on by two presenters. The first presenter gives excellent information but is hundreds of pounds overweight. The second presenter is in outstanding physical shape, has helped thousands of people around the world transform their health, and has a PhD in exercise physiology. They both offer similarly priced coaching programs to continue working with them.

Whose program would you be more inclined to purchase?

The vast majority would choose the second presenter over the first. He looks the part, has the proper credentials, and has a proven track record, each of which helps establish him as an authority figure.

When I first started my business offering B.E.S.T. treatments out of my house, I couldn't understand why people were unwilling to pay me for my services. I was certified and credentialed in an absolutely amazing healthcare technique that helped eliminate pain and stress from the body. Those that came reported outstanding results. Why, then, was I not attracting paying clients?

It finally hit me; no one saw me as an authority figure when I offered treatments in my living room.

This changed when I began renting office space from existing chiropractic clinics, and further changed after giving thousands of treatments, writing several best-selling books, creating dozens of audio trainings, having a proven track record of success, teaching at Harvard University, appearing several times on television and in podcasts, and posting hundreds of client testimonials. Each one of these helped establish me as an authority figure.

"So, Eric, does that mean if I've never been featured in a podcast, written a book, or appeared on television, I can't be seen as an authority figure?"

No, but getting your name out there and heading in that direction wouldn't hurt.

6) Scarcity

Do you remember when Hostess Cupcakes announced it was going out of business a number of years ago? There were people that sold Twinkies on eBay for $5,000.00 apiece, and people were buying them at that price!

Why?

Because there was a *scarcity*.

This is why many promotional materials say, "Limited time offer." When we believe we can have something any time we wish, we often don't take action to obtain it.

My wife is a wonderfully talented massage therapist, but because I can get her massages "any time," I rarely do. It is important to create some sort of scarcity so potential buyers take immediate action.

7) Reason

The student center of a major university had only one photocopy machine. During busy times each day, there was often a forty-five to sixty-minute wait in line to use it.

Imagine yourself standing in such a line, anxiously waiting your turn and hoping to make it to your next class on time when someone approaches you just as you make it to the front of the line.

"May I cut in front of you and use the machine?" they ask.

What would be your response?

You've just waited a full hour for your turn. There are people lined up behind you. Who does this person think they are skipping the line? Why don't they wait their turn like everyone else?

As I'm sure you can understand, most people would be inclined to say no in such a scenario …

... unless that person presented a specific *reason* for wanting to cut in line.

A study done at that same university revealed that approximately 75% of those approached by someone asking, "May I cut in line?" said no, but over 90% of those approached said yes when given a reason for the person to cut in line.

This was especially true when they used the word "because."

"May I cut in line because I am late for class?"

"Sure!"

Even when the reason itself seemed absolutely ridiculous, the percentage of people who responded affirmatively was significantly higher when presented with a reason that used the word "because."

"May I cut in front of you because I really would like to cut in front of you?"

"Sure."

Again, the magic word is "because."

Isn't that interesting?

8) Asked

Have you ever failed to get a date with a special someone, a promotion at work, a sale, or a gift simply because you didn't ask for it?

When you don't ask for something, the answer is going to be no.

If you *do* ask, especially using the skills you are learning in this book, chances are much higher the answer will be yes!

The lives of many people would be dramatically different if they simply asked for what they desired.

What have you been unwilling to ask for?

Answer the following in your persuasion journal:

Up to this point in my life, I have been unwilling to ask for ...

This is affecting my life in the following ways ...

What is keeping you from asking for what you truly desire? How much further ahead would you be if you simply *asked?*

In your persuasion journal, make a firm commitment to yourself to ask for whatever you wrote down by a specific date at a specific time. Also, set a consequence for yourself if you fail to do so. This is something that ought to be so dreadful that you want to avoid it at all costs. (Obviously be safe about it; I am *not* suggesting cutting off a limb or anything like that.)

Also set a reward for yourself when you *do* ask, regardless of the outcome. This ought to be something that will give you so much pleasure that you would absolutely *love* to experience it (again, please be safe and use common sense). This commitment is to be written as follows:

I 100% commit to asking _____ (person/people) for _____ (a raise, a date, a sale, etc.) by _____ (day) at _____ (time). If I do not, I commit to _____ (consequence) by _____ (day) at _____ (time). When I do, I will reward myself with _____ (reward).

Share this commitment with a trusted loved one or accountability partner, including your consequence and reward. Make sure they hold you to your commitment.

Now place your hand over your heart and declare, "I am a master of persuasion!"

"OK, Eric, I get that I need to be better at asking for what I want in life, but is there a way to improve how I present my ideas to others?"

Yes!

The Unsolicited Message

Him: Hey Eric,

I wanted to share this with you because if someone hadn't told me about the *** program, I wouldn't be where I am today! Check this quick video out and let me know if you're interested! :)

Me: Hi ____. If you don't mind me asking, how many enrollments have you had from sending out this message?

Him: You're the first person I sent it to hah. Just made the video 5 min ago!

Me: I see. Would it be safe to assume you want to be as success-ful with it as possible?

Him: You'd be very safe in that assumption.

Me: Cool. Would you be open to some feedback from someone who is a self-made millionaire, multiple-time best-selling author, and international sales trainer?

Him: Sure why not!

Me: Thank you. The very first (and most important) step to making any sort of sale or enrollment is finding out what your prospect's needs are and how/if what you have to offer can fill that need. Did you ask me any questions to find out what needs I might have before sending me a link?

Him: Ahhhh you're absolutely right. I kinda jumped the gun there! I just knew that you were an amazing energetic practitioner and thought it might be something you were interested in..

(Insert commentary: How many times have you received mes-sages like the one above? How many times have you *sent* mes-sages like that? It is extremely common among new network market-ers. They join a network marketing company and (naturally) want to be as successful as possible. They see successful influencers and think, "If I can just get so-and-so on board, they would promote this to all *their* people, and I'll be an overnight success!")

Me: Did I give you any indication at all that I needed or wanted what you are offering?

Him: You did not

Me: Since you didn't find out anything about what I need, want, or am looking for, wouldn't you agree that me taking time away from my own business, seeing clients, writing books, and nurturing my wife and children to look at your business would only help you and not me? Here is what sending out messages like the one you sent does: it sends a message out that says, "I don't care what you want, need, or are doing right now. Stop what you are doing and buy my stuff! Just buy my stuff!"

As an entrepreneur, your job is to find the problem that people have and SOLVE THOSE PROBLEMS. Once you have established a need, desire, or problem you can solve, the next step is ASKING PERMISSION to share a possible solution.

Him: I mean, that's totally fair. I'd agree.

Me: Why would it be important to ask permission before sharing a possible solution?

Him: To see if they're even open to the possibility I'd say rather than just ramming something in their face haha

Me: You are correct.

(End of conversation)

Thirty seconds.

Thirty seconds to determine if someone will like you, buy from you, do business with you, go out with you, and more.

If you only have thirty seconds to make a lasting impression, how can you be sure to make it count?

The answer is simple: master the *six steps of effective networking.*

Step 1: Ask questions to find a *need* or *strong desire.*

Imagine sitting at home, minding your own business, when you hear a knock at your door. When you open it, you see a man in a white coat who introduces himself as Dr. Brown and begins listing the features and benefits of a new "miracle drug" he just invented that would instantly cure athlete's foot that you could purchase from him right then for $500.

What would be the first thoughts that would cross your mind?

Unless you had a serious case of athlete's foot that other treatments had failed to get rid of, you would probably say, "No, thank you," and would want to get back to doing whatever you were doing.

Sadly, this is exactly the approach most people use when trying to make a sale.

They believe if they can tell as many people as possible about all the features and benefits of their products or services, eventually someone will want to buy them.

They fail to realize that people usually don't make purchases unless the product or service fills a *need* or *strong desire.*

The best sales professionals in the world are like excellent physicians. When you go to a doctor's office for a medical issue, he or she will probably ask you several questions to get an idea of what the problem is. Once the problem is identified (the need), the doctor writes a prescription or makes recommendations to correct the problem.

Write the following in your persuasion journal:

The first step in effective networking is identifying a need or strong desire. This is accomplished by asking questions.

Now place your hand over your heart and declare, "I am a master of persuasion!"

Step 2: Ask permission to share a possible solution.

The fact that your prospective clients have expressed a need or strong desire doesn't automatically mean they are looking for a solution. They may simply be looking to vent or find someone to talk to. Offering a solution when someone isn't looking for one can break rapport.

Let's say you help people overcome depression, and the person you are talking to has expressed feeling extremely depressed over the last few days. You found a need. Simply saying, "I totally get how difficult battling depression can be. May I share a possible solution?" can make all the difference.

If they respond, "No, thank you," do not proceed.

This can be extremely difficult for those who struggle with a *Savior Complex* (more about that in Chapter 5).

Some people, out of the goodness of their hearts, can't stand to see other people suffering, and take it upon themselves to try to prevent this from happening. They believe it is their duty to *fix* others when it may not be their responsibility to do so. This can be especially difficult if it is a close friend or loved one who is suffering, particularly when a solution seems extremely obvious.

As difficult as this may be to accept, it is not your responsibility to fix everyone. You are here to help and serve the people you came here to help and serve. If someone isn't willing to accept your help, that's OK. It is their choice, and you must be 100% OK with it. Can that be easier said than done? Yes, but you cannot want to solve someone else's problem more than they want their problem to be solved.

Write the following in your persuasion journal:

I always ask permission before sharing solutions. It is not my responsibility to "fix" or "save" the entire planet. I only proceed once I have permission.

Now place your hand over your heart and declare, "I am a master of persuasion!"

Only proceed to step 3 once permission has been given to share your possible solution.

Step 3: Offer an "out."

This means offering a chance for your prospective client to say no, and showing that you are OK if that takes place. Phrases such as:

"I don't know if this would work for you, but …"

"I don't know if this is what you're looking for, but …"

"I don't know if this would be helpful, but ..."

"I don't know if this is the solution you're looking for, but ..."

"I don't even know if this would be beneficial to you or not, but ..."

This may seem counterintuitive. Why would you want to offer an out?

When you are 100% OK hearing no, it is much more likely your prospects will say yes.

Offering an "out" creates an atmosphere of safety and shows respect for your prospect's individual circumstances.

Write the following in your persuasion journal:

I am 100% OK if my prospect says no. By offering an "out," I am more likely to hear yes!

Now place your hand over your heart and declare, "I am a master of persuasion!"

Step 4: Elevator pitch.

This is a concise statement that clearly communicates the purpose of what you offer, usually no more than about three sentences, and hooks your prospect's attention. Make sure to mold your elevator pitch to match the specific need your prospect mentions. If your prospect says they have "XYZ problem," and you tell them you solve "ZYX problem" with a particular solution, you might break rapport. As close to XYZ problem as ZYX problem might sound to you, it may not seem like the same thing to your prospect. For example, if your prospect tells you, "I need to get rid of my sugar addiction so I can lose 25 pounds within 3 months and fit into my skinny jeans," and, during your elevator pitch, you say, "I help people get rid of 25 pounds within 90 days by overcoming their sugar addictions," as close as those two sentences might be, it isn't exactly what your prospect said they needed. A more effective elevator pitch would be, "I help people get rid of their sugar addiction so they can lose 25 pounds within 3 months and fit into their skinny jeans." If you are corresponding with a prospect via the written word (e.g., email, social media, text, etc.), use the same spelling, wording, word order, punctuation, and abbreviations your prospect uses.

Ask a question at the end of your elevator pitch to gauge interest, such as "Would that be helpful?" or "Would that be of benefit to you?"

Do *not* ask "Is that something you would be interested in?" We will discuss this further in Chapters 4 and 7.

If your prospect responds positively, continue to step 5.

Step 5: Invitation to learn more.

While there are certainly exceptions to this, most people won't consider making a purchasing decision within sixty seconds of meeting you without more information and further developing trust in you and what you offer. Inviting your prospect to learn more (for free) allows them to do exactly that.

What are ways you could invite your prospect to learn more?

- Inviting them out to lunch
- Phone interview
- Zoom interview
- Seminar
- Initial treatment
- Coaching session

Keep in mind that the most effective invitations to learn more include offering your prospect some sort of value up front. When you invite your prospect out to lunch, your prospect gets a free meal regardless of whether or not you do business together. If you offer your prospect a free coaching session, they get tremendous value up front, regardless of whether or not you do business together. This allows them to "test drive" you and what you have to offer so they can make an informed decision regarding whether or not to move forward and activates the law of reciprocity (as discussed earlier in this chapter).

Also keep in mind that most people like to make purchases but strongly dislike feeling "sold to." If they believe your sole intention is to sell them something, they will probably turn down the invitation to learn more. Certain phrases can trigger this feeling, such as:

- "No obligation"
- "Strategy session"
- "Discovery call"
- "Consultation"

When a prospect hears those phrases, they usually think your invitation to "learn more" will be nothing more than a sales pitch. Instead, offer something of value (e.g., lunch, a coaching session, an audio book to listen to before your conversation, etc.), find a date and time that works for both of you, and proceed to step 6.

Step 6: Double Commitment.

This is when you ask for a second confirmation that the date and time you scheduled definitely works for them, and that they will honor and respect your time.

"I'm sure I'm totally preaching to the choir with you, but any time I set aside time in my calendar, I always make sure it is set in stone. If I put you down for ____ (date) at ____ (time), will you 100% for sure be there?"

This is a way to tactfully communicate that your time is valuable and needs to be respected. It honors no one to schedule a meeting, phone call, or other form of allowing your prospect to learn more if he or she isn't going to actually do so.

Asking for a double confirmation will *dramatically* reduce your no-shows and last-minute cancellations. If your prospect responds with anything besides a firm "Yes," do *not* schedule the meeting. If they say, "Well, I don't have anything else in my calendar right now, so go ahead and pencil me in for now, and I'll let you know if something comes up ahead of time," do *not* schedule the meeting. Again, this step helps to eliminate unnecessary no-shows and establishes your prospect's level of commitment. If they are *not* actually interested in what you have to offer, it will often become evident during this step.

If your prospect says something like, "I'll let you know if I can't make it," reaffirm what you already told them about only putting things in your calendar if they are set in stone.

"I appreciate the fact that you would do that. As I mentioned, I only put things in my calendar if they are 100% set in stone. If there is any hesitancy, please tell me now. Is there any hesitancy?"

At this point, your prospect will usually do one of three things:

1. Recommit and let you know they will for sure be there. In this case, go ahead and put it in your calendar and make it happen.
2. Let you know they aren't actually interested. Be thankful you found this out now before you set aside time in your calendar that would have been wasted and taken away from a more productive activity. If this is the case, respond, "Oh, why is that?" You can proceed to overcome objections (more about that in Chapter 7) and schedule the meeting or cancel it altogether.
3. Let you know they are interested but may have a conflict. If this is the case, ask, "What would be a day and time that would work better for you?" Find a new date and time they can for sure commit to, get a double commitment, and make it happen.

Do *not* skip this step!

Don't be afraid of offending people. Throughout all my years in business and asking for double commitments, I can count the number of people who chose to take offense on one hand. Most people are actually impressed when you do this and respect the fact that you show integrity when it comes to your time and the time of others. If someone chooses to be offended by you making sure your time will be respected, it is likely a sign they planned to no-show the appointment. *Always* get a double commitment.

Write the following in your persuasion journal:

When scheduling first-time appointments, I always get a double commitment.

Now place your hand over your heart and declare, "I am a master of persuasion!"

Here's what this might look like in real life (based on an actual conversation held via Facebook Messenger).

Me: Hi, _____ (so-and-so). I saw your post mentioning you were struggling with some health issues. Did you find the answers you were looking for?

Her: Hi, Eric. I received a lot of referrals but haven't made a decision yet. Did you have a recommendation?

Me: I might. May I ask a little about what has been going on?

Her: I suffer from depression. I've been on medication for years. It worked well, but for the last 6 months it hadn't. My Dr. won't change me to a different med. When I up my dose I feel shaky, but the depression does lessen. But I don't like the shaky feeling. That is my concern. I also have diabetes, sleep apnea, and PCOS, so I need help with those as well.

Me: Got it. May I share a possible solution?

Her: Yes, please.

Me: Do you still live in _____ (city)?

Her: Yes.

Me: I don't know if this would help, but I have connections with practitioners that specialize in helping people overcome depression and sleep apnea. They use a technique similar to chiropractic but without the cracking or popping (they get better results that way), and they do more than align the spine. They do that, of course, and they update the part of your nervous system that controls your sleeping patterns and release the stress your body is holding onto, leaving you feeling amazing. It works wonders for depression. I can probably get you in to see one at no charge. Would that be helpful?

Her: Yes, that would help. Don't take this the wrong way, but how?

Me: I own a healthcare company and can pull some strings. What is your schedule usually like on Thursdays?

Her: That's very thoughtful. My schedule is usually flexible on Thursdays.

Me: Could you come in this Thursday, June 11, at 12:30 p.m.?

Her: Yes, that should work.

Me: Cool. What is the best phone number in case we need to reach you before then?

Her: ***-***_****. Where will the appointment be?

Me: The address is _____. And I'm sure I'm totally preaching to the choir with you, but any time we set aside time in our calendar, we always make sure it is set in stone. If we put you down for Thursday, June 11, at 12:30 p.m., will you 100% for sure be there?

Her: Yes, I will be there. Thank you.

Me: Great. See you then.

Write the six steps of effective networking in your persuasion journal:

1. Ask questions to establish a need or strong desire
2. Ask permission to share a possible solution
3. Give an out ("I don't know if … but …")
4. Elevator pitch that ends with a question ("Would that be helpful?")
5. Invitation to learn more
6. Double commitment

Now write the following commitment:

I always follow the six steps of effective networking.

Now place your hand over your heart and declare, "I am a master of persuasion!"

"This is fantastic, Eric. But are there certain phrases that can make a person less likely to accept an invitation to learn more, even if I've followed the six steps of effective networking?"

Yes!

If you aren't careful, you can trigger your prospect's *salesman alarm*.

CHAPTER 4

THE SALESMAN ALARM

D id you ever have an experience as a child of hearing your mom or dad answer the phone (this was before everyone had cell phones with caller ID), only to scream, "Don't ever call this home again!" and proceed to slam the phone onto the receiver? This confused you because your parents taught you to be kind and respectful to others, so you asked what happened, only to hear, "Oh, it was a *salesman!*" What did that teach you about salespeople?

Answer the following prompts in your persuasion journal:

Selling is ...

Salespeople are all ...

When I believe someone is trying to sell me something, I feel ...

Write down the first thoughts that come to your mind.

When I teach my live Master of Persuasion seminars and invite audience members to share what they write, most people have several negative feelings toward selling, salespeople, and feeling "sold to," many of which stem from experiences in their childhood similar to the one above.

Most people have a *salesman alarm* in their subconscious mind that acts like a sixth sense and gets triggered when they feel they are being sold to. Certain phrases, gestures, and actions can trigger the salesman alarm.

The greatest salespeople in the world regularly sell high-ticket products and services with ease and never once trigger the salesman alarm.

Masters of persuasion modify their language, body language, and facial expressions just enough to make large transactions happen without ever causing their prospects to feel sold to.

Consider the following question asked two different ways. Pay attention to how you would feel if someone you just met approached you on the street and asked you this question:

"Excuse me, would you be interested in earning one hundred million dollars right now?"

What would be the first thought to cross your mind?

Would you automatically say yes?

Would you be skeptical?

Would you be inclined to turn down the offer without finding out more details?

When I pose this question to my live audiences, over ninety percent of the room respond feeling skeptical and would probably turn the offer down.

"Why would you turn it down?" I ask. "It could be a completely legitimate offer. You could be speaking to an extremely benevolent multibillionaire who just happens to be doing a social experiment and is giving away one hundred million dollars to the first person willing to receive it."

The audience usually responds that something in that question just seems *off*.

I then ask the same question phrased a little differently:

"Would it be OK if you earned one hundred million dollars?"

When I ask the audience how they would respond to that question, it is almost always unanimous; nearly everyone always says yes without hesitation.

What made the difference?

A number of years ago, when the network marketing industry was young, many of the first people who signed up as distributors were taught to use a certain phrase when prospecting. This phrase has since become synonymous with salespeople, so most people automatically say no when they hear it, regardless of who uses it or what follows it. The phrase is:

"Would you be interested in …"

This phrase nearly always triggers the salesman alarm and, when used, nearly always elicits a negative response.

If you want to be a master of persuasion, cut that phrase out of your vocabulary.

"So what phrase can we use instead?"

My wife had the privilege of attending a training led by a gentleman named Tom "Big Al" Schreiter, who promised to teach five words that would change each attendee's life (this entire chapter is based on his training).

That evening, my wife taught these words to me.

I was working as a server in a Brazilian steakhouse at the time. A Brazilian steakhouse is very different from a traditional steakhouse where a server takes your order, the cooks cook it, you eat it, pay, and leave.

Brazilian steakhouses offer all-you-can-eat meat.

After sitting down at your table, a server will welcome you, take your beverage order, and explain that every couple of minutes, meat servers will come by the table and offer you a different cut of meat. You may have as much or as little as you would like; it is all included in the price of the meal.

At the restaurant where I worked, there were a number of items guests could add to their meal for an additional charge, such as scallops or lobster tails. The price of the full meal was $24 per adult for dinner, and a single lobster tail was an additional $30. Most servers sold one or two lobster tails per year, believing that no one would want to spend the extra money since they were already paying a significant amount for an all-you-can-eat experience.

After learning the five words that could change my life, I decided to try an experiment.

Utilizing these five words, I didn't sell one lobster tail in twelve months; I sold *fifty* lobster tails in just over two months.

Eleven of those lobster tails happened to be to a sales office that offered me a position selling alarm systems that summer (I accepted), which put me on a trajectory to starting my own company and becoming a millionaire by age 30.

Five words literally changed my life.

"OK, Eric, enough talk! What are the five words!?!"

1. Would
2. It
3. Be
4. OK
5. If …

From that moment on, I used these five words with every party I served.

After writing down their drink order, I asked, "Would it be OK if I shared a few tips to make the most out of your experience here today?"

Most people gratefully said, "Yes!"

"In addition to delicious meats and salads you'll be enjoying today, we have a few additional menu items we can add to enhance your meal for an additional charge that most people find gives them the absolute best experience possible here, including ten-ounce lobster tails that are gently steamed, served with butter and fresh lemon, and are absolutely to die for! I can't recommend them enough. Would it be OK if you had the best possible experience tonight and enjoyed one?"

Think back to the same question asked two different ways:

"Would you be interested in earning one hundred million dollars?"

"Would it be OK if you earned one hundred million dollars?"

The first phrase ("Would you be interested in ...") triggers the salesman alarm.

The second phrase ("Would it be OK if ...") does not.

What might be examples of other ways you could use these five words?

"Would it be OK if you tripled your income?"

"Would it be OK if you eliminated your back pain?"

"Would it be OK if you dramatically improved your marriage?"

"Would it be OK if you no longer had to work for a living?"

"Would it be OK if you replaced your depression with peace, happiness, and fulfillment?"

In your persuasion journal, write down a list of at least five additional questions you could ask that pertain to your particular business, starting with "Would it be OK if ..."

Now place your hand over your heart and declare, "I am a master of persuasion!"

Want to take this concept to another level?

Replace "OK" with words such as "helpful," "beneficial," "valuable," and the like, such as:

"Would it be helpful if I connected you with a specialist who could treat you at no charge?"

"Would it be beneficial to you if your office was organized for you?"

"Would it be valuable for someone to mow your lawn for you every week so you can focus on more productive and lucrative tasks?"

"This concept makes sense, Eric. Are there other actions or phrases that trigger the salesman alarm?"

Yes!

The "Salesman Smirk"

After presenting products I had for sale, someone once told me, "Eric, these products are fantastic, but I don't want to buy them from *you*. If they were available at the supermarket, I'd go buy them immediately!"

"How rude," I thought! "Why would this 'friend' be willing to fill the pockets of the supermarket owners but not be willing to help me support my wife and children?"

Most people who try their hand at sales think this way in the beginning. They get frustrated when their friends and family members are unwilling to support them by purchasing from them. What they don't realize is most people enjoy *purchasing* but strongly dislike being *sold*.

The *salesman smirk* is a very small smile (usually no more than the slightest upturn of one corner of the mouth) that occurs when a person thinks about how he or she will benefit from someone purchasing from them (i.e., financially). It nearly always triggers the salesman alarm because we tend to be an extremely cautious society. If we believe someone's intention is only to benefit himself or herself and not us, we are quick to say no.

This is why it is absolutely critical when presenting an offer to a prospect (particularly when discussing the price) to have a *pleasant but neutral countenance*. As ridiculous as it may seem, appearing too happy or excited about a sale can cause prospects to think they are getting the short end of the stick.

If thoughts cross your mind of how much money you will receive by making the sale, immediately replace them with compliments and love for your prospect.

Write the following in your persuasion journal:

I keep a pleasant but neutral countenance when making offers to prospects. If a thought about money crosses my mind, I immediately replace it with love and compliments for my prospect.

Now place your hand over your heart and declare, "I am a master of persuasion!"

Talking Too Much

"If I can spew enough facts, features, and benefits about my product, something *has* to catch their attention, and they will want to buy!"

That ridiculous thought actually crossed my mind when I first began my sales career.

Unfortunately, the same thought crosses the minds of most amateur salespeople and network marketers.

Does this work?

Absolutely not!

When it comes to sales, less is always more, meaning you talk *less* and allow your prospect to talk *more*. Spend most of the time asking questions to identify your prospect's root needs and determine how your product or service can fill that need. Avoid the temptation to give more information than you are asked to give. It is very easy to talk a prospect *out* of purchasing by talking too much.

When you *do* talk, keep to the point and ask your prospect engaging questions every few sentences, such as:

"Does that make sense?"

"Are you with me?"

"Would that be helpful?"

"Does that match what you are looking for?"

"What kind of difference would that make?"

"How would that feel?"

"How does that sound so far?"

Make sure to base your questions on your prospect's individual buying strategy (more on that in Chapter 5).

Write the following in your persuasion journal:

When it comes to talking, less is more. I only share as much information as I am asked to share. Every few sentences, I ask a question to keep my prospect engaged.

Now place your hand over your heart and declare, "I am a master of persuasion!"

Speaking Too *Quickly*

People tend to speak faster than normal when nervous. Speaking too quickly during a presentation can cause your prospects to lose trust in you because they assume you must not be as knowledgeable or confident as you ought to be if you truly were an expert in whatever you are presenting. It causes you to appear desperate. Remember: desperation energy will ruin nearly any sale.

Think of a wise old guru, someone whom you *know that he knows.* If you asked him a question, how would he respond? What would his demeanor be like? How quickly or slowly would he speak?

Experts tend to exude a confident energy which causes them to be more still and speak more slowly, calmly, and collectedly. When presenting, slow down, enunciate your words, speak from your heart. You can still be animated and passionate, but pay attention to your word speed.

Write the following in your persuasion journal:

Experts are calm, collected, and confident. I am seen as an expert when I speak more slowly.

Now place your hand over your heart and declare, "I am a master of persuasion!"

Additional Words and Phrases that Trigger the Salesman Alarm

"Opportunity"

This word is often linked with network marketing parties. Replace it with "get-together" (e.g., "Would you be willing to bring napkins to my get-together this Saturday?")

"Contract"

Replace this word with "agreement" or "paperwork." (e.g., "I'll start filling out the paperwork.")

"Signature"

Replace this with "autograph" (e.g., "Please autograph and date at the bottom of this page.")

"Pay"

Replace this with "take care of" (e.g., "How would you like to take care of this today?")

"Eric, if there are phrases that nearly always trigger the salesman alarm, are there other phrases that *never* do?"

Yes!

"Everyone knows ..."

What goes through your mind when you hear this phrase? Most people have a thought process that goes something like, "Everyone knows this? I'm included in 'everyone.' This must be a true statement!"

Examples may include:

"Everyone knows that reading and applying *Master of Persuasion* will dramatically improve your life."

"Everyone knows that healthy eating and exercise can improve your overall health."

"Everyone knows that people who join XYZ network marketing company become millionaires within three to five years."

Make a list of five additional "Everyone knows" phrases that pertain to your specific product or service in your persuasion journal.

Now place your hand over your heart and declare, "I am a master of persuasion!"

"Most people ..."

Similar to "everyone knows," this phrase uses social proof. Our natural tendency is to want to be part of the majority. Examples may include:

"Most people who stay in this hotel room reuse their towels at least once."

"Most people who book a reservation at this restaurant order a rose for someone in their party."

"Most people who graduate from Eric Bailey's Successful Mentor program earn a six-figure income their first full year after graduating."

"Most people want to be excellent parents but struggle from time to time."

Make a list of five additional "Most people" phrases that pertain to your specific product or service in your persuasion journal.

Now place your hand over your heart and declare, "I am a master of persuasion!"

"There are two types of people in the world ..."

As soon as most people hear "There are two types of people in the world ...," they automatically pay attention and think, "Which one am I?"

Examples may include:

"There are two types of people in the world: those who work for other people and those who work for themselves."

"There are two types of people in the world: those who have happy marriages and those who do not."

"There are two types of people in the world: those who struggle with their weight and those who have found a way to easily maintain a healthy weight."

Make a list of five additional "There are two types of people in the world" phrases that pertain to your specific product or service in your persuasion journal.

Now place your hand over your heart and declare, "I am a master of persuasion!"

Those who master the art of communicating without triggering the salesman alarm understand that the process of selling can be truly fun and beautiful.

Master of Persuasion

CHAPTER 5

SELLING CAN BE FUN AND BEAUTIFUL!

P hysicians tend to be the greatest salespeople in the world because they follow a simple formula:

1. Ask questions to discover the problem
2. Diagnose the problem
3. Qualification/asking about insurance plans/payment options
4. Make recommendations and/or write prescriptions
5. Tell you how to follow through and/or how to purchase the prescription

Can you imagine a physician thinking, "Is this person going to judge me if I try to sell them this prescription?"

Of course not.

Selling can be extremely simple when you follow the same five-step formula:

1. **Ask questions to uncover a need, problem, or strong desire**
2. **Diagnosis**
3. **Qualification**
4. **Recommendation**
5. **Close**

Consider the following conversation as an illustration of the five steps:

Me: Hi, _____. I saw your post about looking for weight-loss products. Did you find what you were looking for?

Her: Not yet. Several people commented with links to products they sell, but none of them really seem to address my problem.

Me: I see. I actually have several connections to people within the weight-loss industry. May I ask you a few questions to see if I can help?

Her: Sure.

Me: Thanks. First, about how much weight are you hoping to lose?

Her: You know, my doctor tells me I need to lose about 50 pounds or I may be in danger of getting type 2 diabetes.

Me: We certainly don't want that. You mentioned that you saw several products but that none of them really seem to address your problem. What seems to be the problem you are facing?

Her: I'm a stress-eater. I eat really healthy for the whole day and even get some exercise in, but right at night before I go to bed, something almost always stresses me, and I end up overeating a ton right before I go to sleep and sabotaging everything. It's really frustrating!

Me: That would be frustrating. Do you have a "go to" of what you usually end up eating right before you go to bed?

Her: Yes, it's always something with sugar!

Me: Got it. If there was a product that helped to instantly relieve stress and make it so sugar wasn't a temptation for you, what kind of difference would that make for you?

Her: That would make a HUGE difference!

Me: Cool. If such a product existed, how soon would you want it?

Her: As soon as possible! I can't keep living this way!

Me: Understood. I actually do know of a few different products that can do that for you. Some are more expensive than others, but of course you get what you pay for. Are you looking for the least expensive product on the market that may or may not work, or are you looking for quality and something that is proven to help you eliminate stress, eliminate the temptation to eat sugary foods, and help you lose 50 pounds as quickly as possible?

Her: Well, obviously I'm all about saving money, but at this point I'm willing to try just about anything as long as it works.

Me: Got it. Personal question: What is your price range for such a product?

Her: I'm open to just about anything, but if there was something that cost less than $100, that would be ideal.

Me: Cool. I do have something that matches that description. The only thing I need to tell you beforehand, though, is a certain kind of person that this particular product doesn't help. I respect your time too much to waste it. The kind of person this product doesn't work on is the kind of person that isn't really committed to getting results and who uses what I call the "procrastination phrases," such as, "I'll think about it," "Maybe one day, but not now," "I'm just curious," "I have to talk to so-and-so before I do anything," "I have to check my schedule first," or "I have to check my budget first," "I'm going to do some research before getting anything," or basically any other excuse why they don't actually take the action required to get the results they say they want. These are usually the people to whom we say, "Thank you for expressing interest. Unfortunately, these products probably aren't for you." This is because, as I'm sure you can imagine, the only way to get results is to take action, get the products, and of course use them! And the people that use the phrases I mentioned, generally speaking, don't do so, so it ends up not working out for them in the end. I wanted to be up front with you in case there was an issue with any of that before I make recommendations. Is any of that a deal breaker at all?

Her: Not at all. I need to lose this weight and am committed to getting there.

Me: Awesome. Based on what you've told me, I would recommend a product called Sxinney Mist. It is a spray you squirt onto your tongue any time you get stressed or are craving sugar. It does two things: it has a blend of herbs in it that help you calm down and feel less stressed (I call it "chill pill in a bottle"), and it blocks the taste of refined sugar on your tongue for about thirty minutes. If you spray it and then try to eat a piece of chocolate, it will taste like baking cocoa, and you'll spit it right out, which helps to eliminate both your stress and your sugar cravings, which makes losing those fifty pounds much easier. Would that be helpful?

Her: That sounds amazing! Where do I get it?

Me: There are a couple of options: you could go online and order it from the company website if you don't mind paying full price for it, or I actually have a discount code I can offer people since the chairman of the board is a former client of mine. Would you prefer to get it on the website for full price, or for me to help you get it at a discounted rate?

Her: Discounts are always nice!

Me: Cool. The regular price is twenty-nine dollars, but I am able to get it for people for just nineteen. I just need a bit of information from you. What address would you like it shipped to?

Her: Please send it to _____.

Me: Got it. What is your phone number and email address?

Her: _____ and _____.

Me: Perfect. Now it just asks for a card number. Go ahead as soon as you are ready.

Her: It's _____.

Me: Thank you. What is the expiration?

Her: _____

Me: Thank you. And the CVV?

Her: _____.

Me: Perfect, thank you. That went through just fine. You should be receiving a confirmation email shortly, and the product should be arriving at your house within the next three days. Do you have any questions or anything else I can help you with?

Her: No, thank you so much!

Me: You're very welcome. And congratulations for being well on your way to losing fifty pounds and becoming a leaner, healthier you!

Her: Thank you so much!

Read through that conversation again, this time marking each of the five steps. Identify the questions, the "diagnosis," qualification, recommendation, and close.

How might you create a similar dialogue with your prospects based on the products and services you offer?

Let's break this down by answering a number of questions in your persuasion journal:

What problems do your products or services solve for people?

What are the challenges that people who have these problems face?

What are specific "symptoms" of people who have these problems?

What happens if these problems aren't solved?

Why would a person who has these problems want a solution?

How would life be better with these problems solved?

Use your answers to these questions to create five or more questions you could ask when uncovering a prospect's problem.

Next, answer the following:

What kind of people do you want to do business with?

What are specific characteristics of your ideal clients?

What are specific characteristics of people you do *not* want to do business with?

Use your answers to these questions to create qualifying questions you could ask before transitioning into the close.

Having a hard time with this one?

Keep in mind that the purpose of asking qualifying questions is to overcome potential objections before they ever come up.

Consider the seven most common objections when creating your qualifying questions:

- No money
- No time
- No need
- No urgency
- No trust
- Indecision (i.e., "Let me think about it.")
- Have to talk to spouse before committing

Read the conversation above one more time and identify how many of the seven most common objections it overcomes.

If your product or service can be classified as "high-ticket," which for most people is anything that costs more than one thousand dollars, the qualification phase may need to be longer than it would be with a lower-ticket item. Purchasing a vehicle that costs one hundred thousand dollars requires more qualifications than purchasing a weight-reduction product that costs nineteen dollars. Does that make sense?

What specific qualifications do your clients need to meet?

Does your product or service require getting a loan?

If so, do your prospects need to have a certain credit score?

Do they need to have access to other resources?

Do they need to be between certain ages?

Do they need to own a business that generates a certain amount of annual revenue?

Do they need to have their spouse present to make a purchasing decision?

In your persuasion journal, make a list of qualifying questions you could ask your potential buyers.

Remember: if your prospects do not meet your list of qualifications, do *not* offer them your product or service.

I'll say that one more time: **If your prospects do not meet your list of qualifications, do *not* offer them your product or service.**

Even if you are desperate for money.

Even if you think you could close them anyway.

Even if your prospect begs you to sell them your product or service.

Trying to close a prospect that does not meet the qualifications of your product or service wastes your time, wastes your prospect's time, and creates a win-lose situation, the very definition of *manipulation*.

If your company requires a 700+ credit score to purchase something from you, and your prospect has a 650 credit score, it will be a waste of time to try to close him; he simply doesn't qualify.

If you sell multimillion-dollar homes, and your prospect barely makes minimum wage, has no savings and no one who could co-sign on a home, do not try to close him; he simply doesn't qualify.

If you sell high-ticket coaching packages over the phone that only benefit quick decision-makers, and your prospect insists several times that she can't make quick decisions, do not try to close her; she simply doesn't qualify.

That doesn't mean these people are bad. It simply means there is another product or service out there that would better suit their specific needs.

Love and respect your prospects enough to not waste their time.

Love and respect *yourself* enough to not waste *your* time.

Have enough love and respect to be 100% OK sending people elsewhere if they fail to meet the qualifications to purchase from you. Period.

Write the following in your persuasion journal:

If someone doesn't meet the qualifications I look for to purchase my product or service, I respectfully refer them elsewhere. I do not have to close everyone. I do not need to or try to close everyone. I am 100% OK closing the right people who need my product or service.

Now place your hand over your heart and declare, "I am a master of persuasion!"

This concept can be extremely triggering for some. There are some who dislike the idea of financial transactions, believing they should help everyone who asks, regardless of their ability to pay. Extreme cases of this are referred to as a *Savior Complex.*

Let me make something extremely clear:

It is not your job to save people. The role of Savior has been filled. There are no openings!

If you are married to someone who works full-time for a company to provide for your family, would you expect your spouse to work for free?

Of course not! Neither should you!

It does *not* make you more spiritual or holy to give away your products, services, time, and talents for free.

This doesn't mean you can't ever be charitable, but here's the deal: you cannot give what you don't have. Sooner or later, if you keep trying to serve people who don't qualify for your products or services by being unable to pay, you are going to burn out. Sooner or later, you are going to run out of products, services, time, energy, and patience. There *must* be an even exchange. Get over any notion in your head that you are obligated to give things away for free if someone "cannot" pay you. If someone wants or needs something bad enough, they will find a way.

Tony Robbins says it is never a matter of resources but a matter of resourcefulness.

You do yourself and your clients an enormous disservice when you take away the chance for them to invest in themselves.

When people *pay*, they tend to *pay attention.*

The more they *invest,* the more *invested* they tend to be.

Write the following in your persuasion journal:

I lovingly send those who don't qualify to receive my products and services elsewhere. I respect myself and my clients enough to receive an equal exchange, including financial transactions.

Now place your hand over your heart and declare, "I am a master of persuasion!"

On the flip side, if your prospect *does* qualify, you have now overcome potential objections before they come up. For example, if your prospect tells you she has $500 saved to invest in a coaching program to teach her how to do online marketing, and you sell a program for $250, you have just overcome the "No money"/"I can't afford it" objection without it ever coming up.

If you insist on speaking with married prospects only when their spouse can be present, you have just overcome the "I have to talk to my spouse before committing" objection without it ever coming up.

If you ask your prospect for a commitment to either tell you, "No, thank you" or "Yes, please" after learning the details of your proposal, you have just overcome the "Let me think about it" objection without it ever coming up.

Write the following in your persuasion journal:

The most effective way to overcome objections is to do so before they ever come up by asking qualifying questions.

Now place your hand over your heart and declare, "I am a master of persuasion!"

Buying Strategies

Now that you've qualified your prospects, you may proceed to make recommendations while utilizing appropriate wording according to your prospects' *buying strategy.*

Everyone has a *buying strategy,* or specific wording that piques their interest and creates a desire to buy. Using the right buying strategy will dramatically increase your closing ratio. Using the wrong buying strategy can talk a very interested prospect out of buying from you.

The latter happened to me when I was in the market for my dream car.

I couldn't believe my eyes.

My 10-year-old self was experiencing love at first sight.

There, right in front of me, was a brand-new, shiny black Chevrolet Corvette convertible.

My jaw dropped as the owner, dressed in all black, the very definition of awesome, stepped out, winked at me, and entered his office building.

"Someday," I thought. "I promise, here and now, that I will own one of those!"

Twenty years later, the time had come.

I walked into the dealership with twenty years of anticipation, twenty years of hard work, growth, and progress, twenty years of looking forward to this day when I could finally buy this car …

… and within thirty seconds, the salesman lost my business …

… simply because he used the wrong buying strategy and literally talked me *out* of purchasing my dream car from him.

Failing to identify and utilize your prospects' buying strategy is a sure-fire way of losing their business.

Masters of persuasion are masters of identifying and utilizing each prospect's individual buying strategy.

The four buying strategies are:
1. Visual
2. Auditory
3. Logical
4. Kinesthetic

Visual

This is someone who needs to *see* things, either literally or figuratively, to make a purchasing decision. These people buy things primarily based on how they *look*. Fliers, brochures, pictures, or videos of your product or service catch their attention. When speaking to a visual person, use words such as:

"Picture this ..."
"Let's take a look at this ..."
"Can you imagine ...?"
"Do you see the solution?"
"What would that look like to you?"
"If everything looks good, can we move forward?"

Make a list in your persuasion journal of five or more phrases that relate to your product or service you could use when speaking with a *visual* person.

Auditory

This is someone who needs to *hear* things, either literally or figuratively, to make a purchasing decision. These people buy things primarily based on how things *sound*. They often appreciate hearing testimonials from satisfied buyers. When speaking to an auditory person, use words such as:

"Listen to this …"

"What are you hearing me say?"

"How does that sound?"

"Listen to this proposal …"

"Tell you what …"

"If I can tell you everything you need to hear, and everything sounds good, can we move forward?"

Make a list in your persuasion journal of five or more phrases that relate to your product or service you could use when speaking with an *auditory* person.

Logical

This is someone who needs things to *make sense* in their mind to make a purchasing decision. These people buy things primarily based on *logic* and are often left-brained. Logical people often appreciate statistics, data, and facts. When speaking to a logical person, use words such as:

"Science has shown …"

"According to statistics …"

"Does that make sense?"

"What would be the logical choice?"

"Why don't we go over the details and numbers, and if everything makes sense, we move forward?"

Make a list in your persuasion journal of five or more phrases that relate to your product or service you could use when speaking with a *logical* person.

Kinesthetic

This is someone who needs to *feel* things, either literally or figuratively, to make a purchasing decision. These people buy things primarily based on how things *feel*. They often appreciate being handed some sort of sample to touch. When speaking to a kinesthetic person, use words such as:

"Do you like the feel of ..."
"How does that resonate?"
"Does this fit together?"
"How would that feel?"
"Why don't we go over the details to determine how they fit together with your goals and, if everything resonates and feels right to you, we move forward?"

Make a list in your persuasion journal of five or more phrases that relate to your product or service you could use when speaking with a *kinesthetic* person.

"So how do I know what my prospect's buying strategy is?"

There are two ways.

The first is through your prospect's *body language.*

If your prospects scratch or rub on or around their *eyes*, they are sending a message that they cannot *see* what you are telling them. Use more *visual* words.

If your prospects scratch or rub on or around their *ears*, they are sending a message that they cannot *hear* what you are telling them. Use more *auditory* words.

If your prospects scratch or rub on or around their *noses*, they are sending a message that they cannot *make sense of* what you are telling them. Use more *logical* words.

If your prospects scratch or rub on or around the *back of their heads* (near the feeling part of the brain), they are sending a message that they cannot *feel* what you are telling them. Use more *kinesthetic* words.

The second way is by simply listening to the words your prospects use to describe the products they hope to purchase and the outcomes they desire to achieve.

"Mr. Prospect, what is it about this kind of car that you like?"

"I love the color and the way I look when driving it!" Visual.

"Mrs. Prospect, what kind of house are you hoping I can help you find?"

"It really comes down to the numbers and what makes sense for our growing family." Logical.

"Mr. Prospect, what are you hoping I can do for you today?"

"I've been in pain for quite some time. If you can help me find a way to feel better and get out of pain, that would be great!" Kinesthetic.

"Mrs. Prospect, what kind of television can I help you find today?"

"Something with outstanding sound. It needs to be better sounding than my old TV!" Auditory.

You get the idea.

"Eric, are some buying strategies more common than others? Is it possible someone can have more than one buying strategy?"

Yes and yes.

Those that graduate from our Master Closer program learn which buying strategies are more common than others and master the art of eliciting their prospects' exact buying strategies to dramatically increase their closing strategies. When properly implemented, the Master Closer program pays for itself again and again and again. More details about that later.

Write the following in your persuasion journal:

I pay attention to the body language and buying strategy of my prospects and use the appropriate wording.

Now place your hand over your heart and declare, "I am a master of persuasion!"

"Eric, I can see how this simplifies the process of making a sale and how asking qualifying questions can reduce the number of objections I have to overcome. What do I do when a prospect still has legit objections?"

The process of overcoming objections can be as simple as anything else when you know how to do it...

Master of Persuasion

CHAPTER 6

HOW TO NEVER HAVE TO HEAR OBJECTIONS AGAIN

M ake a list in your persuasion journal of objections you deal with on a regular basis and/or objections you haven't known how to overcome.

Now put a check mark next to each of the objections listed that you personally use when making purchasing decisions.

How many of them matched?

We tend to attract people into our lives that are like ourselves.

If you are an "I'll think about it" type of person, you are going to attract "I'll think about it" people into your life.

If you regularly tell people, "I can't afford that," you're going to attract people into your life who tell you they can't afford what you offer.

Overcoming objections begins, first and foremost, with *you*. You must become your ideal client.

"Wait, Eric, does that mean I have to say yes to everything that presents itself to me?"

No.

It *does* mean that you honor the time of others, listen to proposals with an open heart and mind, and love others enough to simply tell them, "No, thank you," or "Yes, please," when presented with purchasing options, and follow through with what you say you will do.

Write the following in your persuasion journal:

Overcoming objections starts with me. I attract people into my life that are like me. I 100% commit to becoming my ideal client and treating others the way I wish to be treated.

Now place your hand over your heart and declare, "I am a master of persuasion!"

With that said, consider the following process when overcoming objections becomes necessary.

Step 1: Restate the objection.

Prospect: "I don't have enough money to purchase this right now."

You: "OK. Just to make sure I understand correctly, you are concerned that you don't have enough money to purchase this right now. Did I understand that correctly?"

This allows you to make sure you understand the concern.

Step 2: Find out if there are additional concerns.

"Is that the only concern?"

If the prospect says no, ask, "What are the other concerns?" You want to have all the concerns out in the open.

If the prospect says yes, proceed to step 3.

Step 3: Identify if the objection is a *smoke screen* or a *legitimate concern*.

Smoke screens are excuses prospects make when they don't want to admit the real reason they aren't buying.

For example, if someone didn't want to admit having no money, they might say, "I need to discuss this with my wife."

Smoke screens can be identified by asking the prospect what would happen if there was a solution to their concern.

"If money wasn't a concern at the moment, then what?"

Or

"If you *did* have the money right now, what kind of difference would that make?"

If they proceed with another objection, concern, or procrastination tool, such as, "Well, then I'd think it over," you've probably uncovered a smoke screen.

When this happens, say, "Mr./Ms. Prospect, you won't offend me. What's the *real* concern?"

If they continue to put up smoke screens, proceed with the *take-away approach* (more on that on page 83).

If the prospect indicates they would make the purchase if their concern was resolved, proceed to step 4.

Step 4: Validate the concern

"I totally understand. This *isn't* inexpensive and *does* require some money."

Validating the concern helps your prospect get out of feeling "triggered."

They think, "This person gets me. They're on my side!"

Other phrases you might use here include:

"I totally get where you're coming from. I used to have that same problem!"

"I get it. I know a lot of people who have that same concern."

"I know what you mean. I used to think that way, too."

Never, *ever* contradict or argue with the prospect. It does nothing but break rapport and leaves the prospect angry.

Step 5: Offer a solution to their concern and/or turn their concern into a reason why they could move forward.

"If there was a way for you to get started experiencing the benefits of this service without getting charged until after your next payday, would that make a difference?"

"If financing was available and you didn't have to come up with all the money up front, would that make a difference?"

"Mr. Prospect, if I'm understanding you correctly, your biggest concern is the money it would take to invest in this product. Am I understanding that correctly?"

"That's a very valid concern. Life tends to be expensive sometimes. Something that most people that purchase this product have found is that, when they get this product, it actually *saves* them a significant amount of money in other areas of their life. If I were to show you a step-by-step plan of how to actually use this product to save you a significant amount of money in the long run, would that make a difference for you?"

"I can totally understand the desire to clear up your debt before investing in a coaching program like this. That's exactly why most people *do* invest in this coaching program. Can I ask you a question? If you were to add an extra $100,000 to your annual income, how much easier would it be to pay off your debt? Over eighty percent of our graduates from this coaching program earn $100,000 more each year following their graduation. If investing in this program added an extra $100,000 or more to your annual income and actually made it significantly easier to pay off your debts faster, would that make a difference?"

If the prospect says no, ask what *would* make a difference. Do your best to find a way for your prospect to say yes!

If the prospect persists with a no, consider utilizing a *takeaway approach*.

Takeaway approaches are a way to test the waters with your prospects to see if they truly do want what you are offering. This is when you describe scenarios in which you would *not* offer your product or service to someone.

For example, the practitioners in my clinics let everyone know during their first visit that there are certain kinds of people we will *not* accept as patients, including those who are not 100% dedicated to healing. This becomes evident when people use such phrases as "I'll think about it," "Maybe one day," "I want to see how I feel tomorrow, and I'll 'call you,'" "I have to talk to so-and-so first," "I have to check my schedule first," "I have to check my budget first," or any other excuse for why they aren't achieving the results they say they want. I *only* work with those who are 100% committed to healing and making progress.

If you've never used a takeaway approach before, this may seem scary at first.

Keep in mind that a big part of mastering the art of persuasion is creating win-win situations. Win-win situations cannot be created if anyone's time is wasted.

Respect your prospects' time enough to slice through the garbage, cut to the chase, and determine if what you offer is right for them, or if it would be best to lovingly refer them to someone else.

Write the following in your persuasion journal:

I am a master of persuasion. I create win-win situations by respecting my time and my prospects' time, which sometimes involves using takeaway approaches.

Now place your hand over your heart and declare, "I am a master of persuasion!"

If your prospect responds negatively to your takeaway approach, fantastic. You have just prevented wasting each other's time. End the meeting on a positive note (such as thanking them for their time) and wish them well.

If your prospect responds positively to your takeaway approach and continues to express interest, find the real concern and repeat the process (restate the objection, find out if there are additional concerns, determine if the concern is legitimate or a smoke screen, validate the concern, offer a solution, ask if the solution would make a difference). Continue this process until you find a win-win situation that allows you to both move forward.

A few additional phrases you may find useful when overcoming objections include:

"Oh, why is that?"
   "Have you signed up for the drawing already?"
   "No, I'm not interested."
   "Oh, why is that?"
   "Well, um, I guess I just don't know what it's for."
   "That's OK. Come on over so we can get you entered."

"What do you mean by that? Do you mean this isn't something you want and this is the reason why, or is it that this *is* something you want, and this is simply a concern?"
   This is called *clarifying the intention.*
   Occasionally, a prospect may put up an objection that seems to be a reason why they do not want to move forward. Take this very real conversation as an example:
   "Eric, I'm sure your programs are amazing, but I am currently on welfare. I just don't have a lot of money right now. Plus, I have learning disabilities."

"I see. What is your intention in telling me that? Is it that you would prefer *not* to sign up for this program and these are the reasons why, or is it that you *do* want to do this program, but these are some concerns you have?"

"The latter."

Had I failed to clarify the prospect's intentions, I might have mistaken his objections as reasons for not proceeding to offer him one of my top programs. Thankfully, I asked for clarification, learned he did want to proceed if I could address his concerns, offered him a way to make things work, closed the deal, enjoyed a very nice payday, and helped him transform his life.

"What do you mean?"

"Would you like me to schedule you a time to meet with one of our practitioners?"

"No, that's too expensive."

"What do you mean?"

"Well, I just don't have a lot of extra money right now."

"I totally understand. My reaching out to you was to offer you a gift. There will be no charge for this visit. Would you be willing to receive that gift from me?"

"Wait … Are you sure?"

"Of course."

"Well … OK! Yes! What if I need more visits, though? How much will it be then?"

"Every body is different. Your practitioner will assess your individual situation and make recommendations if further treatments are needed. They are extremely affordable, though. The absolute maximum you will ever pay for a visit is $50."

"Oh, wow, that's not bad at all. Thank you! Yes, let's schedule a visit!"

Tell me more …

"That would take too much time."

"What do you mean?"

"I'm just so busy."

"Tell me more."

"Well, I'm working, caring for grandkids, I'm doing stuff for church, and a little bit of politics."

"It sounds like you do have a pretty full schedule. Is that right?"

"Yes."

"Got it. Let me ask you a question: if I were to help you find a way to utilize this to save you time and actually give you more time to be with your grandkids and spend more time doing what you love, would that make a difference for you?"

"Yeah, that would be great."

"Perfect. If I can do that for you, would you move forward?"

"Yeah."

"Fantastic."

Once you've overcome these objections and created a win-win situation for everyone to proceed, congratulations! You have just arrived at the most important part of the process: **the *close.***

CHAPTER 7

THE CLOSE

Throughout history, the most successful men and women all shared one skill in common: they were all excellent *closers.*

The *close* is when commitments are finalized and transactions take place.

You can be the greatest presenter in the world, but if you don't know how to close, you aren't going to get paid, land that job or promotion, get the date, or change lives by getting your products and services into the hands of those that need them.

Closing is, by far, the most important piece of the persuasion puzzle.

According to *ProSales* Magazine, an average trained and experienced salesperson closes 10–20% of their prospects, while the absolute best salespeople close upwards of 25–50%.

In terms of one-on-one or one-on-two sales, my closing ratio is over 95%, which includes everything from low-ticket items ($99 or less) to high-ticket items (more than $50,000.00). The cost of the service matters very little when you master the art of closing.

There are two kinds of energy that every man and woman possesses: *masculine* and *feminine.*

Regardless of our gender, each of us possesses both kinds of energy.

Masculine energy is the dominant, commanding, go-out-and-get-it-done energy.

Feminine energy is the nurturing, healing, bonding, and attracting energy.

Both kinds of energy have their place in the sales process.

Feminine energy is appropriately used at the beginning of the process as the prospect is nurtured and rapport is built. Asking questions to learn the prospect's needs is typically done in feminine energy.

The close, on the other hand, is done in masculine energy. It makes things happen and gets things done. Masters of persuasion know how and when to shift between masculine and feminine energies.

Unfortunately, some men and women struggle to make the shift, which can make closing the deal extremely difficult.

Those who struggle to shift into feminine energy often come across as overbearing, pushy, and domineering, so they often fail to build the necessary rapport to gain the prospect's trust.

Those who struggle to shift into masculine energy often fear asking for the close, so they never do it.

Have you ever heard someone say they were "nurturing their prospects"? This may be an indicator of someone who struggles to shift out of feminine (nurturing) energy and into masculine (closing) energy.

Again, this has little to nothing to do with the person's gender. I know several women who struggle to step into feminine energy when appropriate and several men who struggle to step into masculine energy when appropriate.

Write the following in your persuasion journal:

The first few steps of the sales process are done in nurturing feminine energy. The last steps of the sales process are done in masculine energy.

Now place your hand over your heart and declare, "I am a master of persuasion!"

"So what can I do if I struggle with switching into masculine energy?"

If this is something you struggle with and you find yourself in a sales presentation, excuse yourself to use the restroom just before you transition into the close.

"Please excuse me while I step away for just a moment. I'll be right back to answer any questions you may have."

Go into the restroom (or a different room where your prospect won't see you) and assume a *power pose.*

Stand up straight, place your feet about shoulder width apart, puff your chest out, hold your arms straight up and out in a V shape (as if you were a football referee signaling a touchdown), and say, "Yes I am! Yes I am! Yes I am!"

Hold this pose for at least thirty seconds.

"That sounds really hokey, Eric. What difference will that make?"

Power poses cause your brain to release testosterone into your body, putting you into masculine energy.

Do this right now.

Come on, stand up right now and assume a power pose. Place your feet about shoulder width apart, puff your chest out, hold your arms straight up and out in a V shape, and say, "Yes I am! Yes I am! Yes I am!"

Hold this pose for at least thirty seconds.

Can you feel the difference?

Most people report feeling empowered, stronger, and more confident after assuming a power pose. This is the energy you need to close the deal.

Once you've completed your power pose, return to your prospect and transition into the close.

"What questions may I answer for you?" is a simple but effective way to transition from the recommendation phase into the close.

A few tips to keep in mind as you make this transition:

Always be seated.

Standing up signifies the end of your meeting. Commitments are made and deals take place when you are seated. Even if your prospect stands up as if to leave, remain seated. If you have built enough rapport, it is likely the prospect will sit back down to match you.

If you excuse yourself to do a power pose, sit back down when you return. Even though the close is done in masculine energy, remaining seated helps ease tension and makes the close more comfortable.

Keep your hands visible but not crossed.

Hands are extremely important in the body language world. Hidden hands send a message to the subconscious that you have something to hide. Since selling has a great deal to do with building rapport and trust, make sure your hands are visible but not crossed in front of you.

Hands crossed form a "protective gate," which sends a message to the subconscious that you want to keep your prospects "out."

Choose the right.

Whenever possible, sit to the right of your prospects. This is another body language tool.

The left side signifies one's past, and the right side signifies one's future. Sitting to your prospect's right sends a message to the subconscious that you are in your prospect's future.

Never ask, "What do you think?"

This one phrase can ruin nearly any sale.

Purchasing decisions take place in the emotional part of the brain. Asking someone what they "think" takes them out of the purchasing part of their brain and puts them into the logical "thinking" part of the brain.

This phrase literally suggests that the prospect "think about the decision" rather than committing and purchasing your product or service.

"Wait a second, Eric. You suggested we ask our prospects if they have any questions. Doesn't that do the exact same thing?"

No.

Asking if your prospects have any questions is a transitional phrase and allows you to uncover any additional concerns or objections they may have.

Asking "What do you think?" takes them completely out of purchasing mode and into thinking mode. Remove this phrase from your vocabulary.

Maintain a neutral countenance.

Keep in mind that most people enjoy purchasing but do not enjoy feeling sold to. If your prospects believe you have something to gain from the transaction (even when it is likely you *do*), they are more likely to say no.

When you are 100% OK with any decision your prospects make, they are much more likely to say yes.

Avoid having a "salesman smirk" and keep your countenance neutral. Immediately replace any thoughts about money with love and compliments for your prospects. You can still be pleasant and animated while remaining neutral.

Utilize *trial closes.*

Trial closes are questions that allow your prospects to say yes in preparation for saying yes at the time of the close. The more your prospects say yes, the more prepared they are to agree to the deal.

Some of my favorite trial closes include:

"If I were to formally extend an offer to receive further treatments here, is this something you would be committed to?"

"If I allowed you into this coaching program, will you utilize it to achieve the results you desire?"

"If I offered you a chance to meet with one of our practitioners at no charge to experience what we do in our clinics, would you receive that gift from me?"

"Would you like to take advantage of the discount we are offering today?"

I usually use one or two trial closes for low-ticket items, and up to five or six for high-ticket items.

If your prospects do *not* respond positively to the trial closes, ask if there are additional concerns they haven't expressed and/or proceed with a takeaway approach.

If they *do* respond positively, proceed to close the deal.

There are dozens and dozens of ways to close a deal. Those that participate in my Master Closer course learn just about every way there is to close any deal. For the purposes of this book, however, here are a few examples of effective closes to get you started:

"How soon would you like this shipped to you?"

"What kind of card would you like to use today?"

"How would you like to take care of (pay for) this?"

"Are you in?"

"Would it be OK if we move forward?"

Practice these closes out loud in front of the mirror until you can easily recite them with a neutral countenance.

Whenever appropriate, ask for payment now.

"How do we want to take care of the down payment today?"

"Will you be using cash, a check, or a card?"

"What kind of card would you like to use?"

Since the world seems to be moving more and more toward using plastic payment methods (i.e., credit and debit cards), the latter is usually my go-to method.

If you can avoid it, do *not* send them an invoice to pay at a later time. It is always best for your prospects to pay immediately following the close. Waiting until later often allows fear and doubt to cloud their judgment, causing them to forget the very reasons they need your life-changing products and services in the first place.

Write the following in your persuasion journal:

Whenever possible, I collect payment immediately following the close.

Now place your hand over your heart and declare, "I am a master of persuasion!"

Taking care of the payment immediately frees up energy; it is one less thing to worry about. Once the payment is made, the deal is done.

Once payment has been collected, fill out any paperwork you need to fill out.

I do *not* recommend filling out paperwork *before* collecting the payment. Doing so gives your client a "chicken exit."

If they don't complete the paperwork, they don't have to make the payment.

If they have already made the payment, they will fill out the paperwork.

In all my years of selling, I have seen a small handful of people refuse to fill out paperwork and thus never make the payment. However, I have *never once* had someone refuse to fill out paperwork *after* making a payment.

Write the following in your persuasion journal:

Whenever possible, I ask for payment immediately after closing the deal and *then* fill out appropriate paperwork.

Now place your hand over your heart and declare, "I am a master of persuasion!"

Once payment has been collected, transition to filling out the paperwork (if appropriate). Since signing paperwork can seem scary to some people, I like to make light of the situation by calling it the "boring legal stuff."

"Thank you so much. We have a little bit of paperwork to fill out, such as consent to be treated. All the boring legal stuff."

After grabbing the proper paperwork and sitting back down, I'll proceed with, "Ready for the boring legal stuff?" with a playful smile on my face.

Some people have weird stigmas about paperwork, so using a bit of playfulness helps lighten any tension that may arise from pulling out documents to sign.

Notice I did *not* say "contract," "signatures," or "agreements." Instead of "signing contracts," we are "filling out paperwork."

After going through the paperwork with your new clients, ask if they have any questions. If they do, answer them. If not, ask them to "autograph" the paperwork (not "sign").

"Any questions?"

"No, everything is pretty straight forward."

"Cool. If you would please autograph and date the bottom and print your name at the top for me. Would you like me to make you a physical copy, or would you prefer to take pictures?"

Once your new clients have autographed and received copies of all the paperwork, smile and congratulate them for making a wise decision.

"Thank you so much, and congratulations for making such a wise decision! Is there anything else I can do for you today?"

Follow up with any instructions on how to receive their products or services and wish them well.

Congratulations! You have just closed the deal!

"Wow, Eric, that really *is* simple. Are there other ways to impact the lives of others besides selling them things?"

Yes!

Masters of persuasion are also outstanding *mentors...*

Master of Persuasion

CHAPTER 8

BECOMING A MENTOR

If you were asked who made the biggest impact in shaping the person you are, how would you respond?

Where would you be in life if no one ever took you under their wing?

Yes, masters of persuasion are excellent at changing lives through sales, getting their life-changing products and services in the hands of others, and making things happen.

Masters of persuasion are also excellent at molding the next generation of influencers.

Masters of persuasion are excellent *mentors.*

Answer the following prompts in your persuasion journal:

The mentors I have had include …

They taught me …

I have benefited from having mentors in the following ways …

Mentors are needed in the world because …

When I ask my live audiences why mentors are important, they usually respond that mentors:

- Help us see our blind spots
- Help us become the people we are meant to be
- Help us keep our commitments
- Help us to see things differently

- Help us believe in ourselves and our dreams

Everyone who achieves any level of excellence has a mentor. Consider that for a moment.

Will you ever meet an Olympic gold medalist who didn't have a coach?

Will you ever hear a musical performance at Carnegie Hall from someone who didn't have a teacher?

Throughout history, the elite have always invested in their family's future by hiring private tutors for their children. As effective as books, audio programs, classes, seminars, and online programs can be, the most effective learning strategy has always been one-on-one mentorship. To reach excellence, it is critical that you have a mentor.

Write the following in your persuasion journal:

To reach excellence, I always have a mentor.

Now place your hand over your heart and declare, "I am a master of persuasion!"

As important as it is for you to always *have* a mentor to become a master of persuasion, it is equally important to learn to *be* an effective mentor.

Success in any area of life comes down to two things:

1. Mechanics/how-to/what to do
2. Mindset/how a person thinks/*why* do it

Likewise, there are two kinds of mentors:

1. The how-to mentor, meaning someone to show you, step by step, how to achieve specific results, also known as *consultants.*
2. The mindset mentor, meaning someone to help you discover answers from within your own mind and hold you accountable, also known as *coaches.*

I've had the privilege of serving as both. Some clients hire me to personally mentor them to achieve some of the things I've achieved, such as:

- Increasing closing ratio to over 90%
- Writing and publishing books and becoming a best-selling author
- Releasing 75+ pounds
- Starting and growing a mentoring/coaching business to 6+ figures
- Overcoming addiction
- Rekindling the flame of a dying relationship
- Starting and growing a healing business to 6+ figures
- Becoming a millionaire

Others work with me to overcome their internal struggles, such as fear, doubt, and self-sabotage.

As important as the how-to is, 80% of success comes from how a person *thinks*.

How you *think* influences what you *believe*. What you *believe* influences your *actions*. Your *actions* influence your *results*.

Someone who *thinks* becoming wealthy isn't worth the struggle and *believes* money is the root of all evil will probably never take the *actions* necessary to *become wealthy*.

Someone who *thinks* the process of releasing fifty pounds of body fat will be overly painful and *believes* the process won't be worth it will probably never take the *actions* necessary to *reach their ideal weight*.

Conversely, someone who *thinks* like a champion, *believes* all things are possible, and takes consistent *action* toward their goals will probably *achieve considerable success*.

The purpose of this chapter is to give you a few basic tools to help yourself, your prospects, your team, your employees, and others within your influence to always be better.

The first rule of effective mentoring is to replace any *judgment* with *unconditional love*.

Mentoring is not the time or place to judge those whom you are mentoring.

When people give you permission to mentor them, you are given a certain level of *stewardship* over them, which allows you to receive *inspiration* for them.

Mentoring is 90% inspiration.

When I teach my live Master of Persuasion seminar, I invite each participant to partner with someone they do not know. I explain that, for a few minutes, they will have the privilege of mentoring their partner with the condition that their partner gives full permission for them to do so. I explain that one partner will have 3–5 minutes to discuss an area of their life where they are struggling. Following this, the other partner will have 5–10 minutes to serve as a mentor and help overcome the struggles their partner shared.

Before the exercise begins, I often see looks of concern from those who have never done this.

"How can I possibly mentor someone I don't even know?"

"How will I know what to say to help them overcome their struggle?"

"What if it's a struggle I have never personally experienced?"

I remind them to replace any judgment they might have with unconditional love and allow themselves to receive inspiration on what to say and do.

"Simply look your partner in the eyes and say whatever you feel impressed to say."

The results of this exercise are always miraculous.

Participants are amazed at their partner's ability to say exactly what they need to hear and at their own ability to do exactly what they need to do to help their partner overcome their struggle.

Write the following in your persuasion journal:

The first rules of becoming an effective mentor are replacing any judgment with unconditional love and allowing myself to receive inspiration regarding what to say and do to help others.

Now place your hand over your heart and declare, "I am a master of persuasion!"

With that said, the following are ten specific mentoring tools you can use to help people achieve greater results. Since this book has to do with persuasion and sales, and there are many who struggle with the fear of selling, the first few have to do with overcoming fear and moving past personal limitations. I strongly encourage you to become your own client the first time you read through these and do the exercises in your persuasion journal.

1. The Root Fear

The fears we feel are often just surface distractors that deter us from what we really fear underneath.

The way to find the actual underlying root fear is by asking your clients to share what their biggest fear is.

Let's say that they respond that their biggest fear is failure. Ask them, "What would be the worst part about failure?"

They may respond that failure would mean they had disappointed their parents.

Ask them, "What would be the worst part about disappointing parents?"

Continue to do this until your clients draw a blank and can't think of anything else. This may take a few minutes, and occasionally the clients may go in circles.

Be patient with your clients during this process and keep at it until they draw that blank or say, "That's it." You have now found the underlying root fear and can proceed to help your student overcome it using another tool in this chapter.

2. Scale of 1 to 10

Most fears come from the emotional side of the brain.

A simple, yet highly effective tool for removing the energetic charge of fear is inviting your clients, anytime they begin to feel a certain fear, to ask themselves how strongly they feel the fear on a scale of 1 to 10.

The act of measuring their fear puts them back into the logical side of their brain where fear doesn't exist.

3. Fear-to-Funny Technique

I had a very vivid nightmare when I was six years old that kept me up at night for years.

In the nightmare, I was observing a group of young children playing near the edge of a tall, jagged cliff. They kept getting closer and closer to the edge which, if they fell off, would lead to their death. I kept wanting to shout at the children to not get any closer because something bad was going to happen if they did, but they couldn't hear me.

For years, I would close my eyes to sleep at night, and the image of the cliff would come into my mind, bringing with it the fear that accompanied it.

That happened until, one night, I decided to do something I had never done before.

In my mind, I gave the cliff a funny-looking face and imagined that, any time someone came near it, it would say, "Hi there! How ya doin'?"

It was now a friendly cliff, and a friendly cliff could do no harm!

I never had that nightmare again.

Any time the image of the cliff would begin to pop into my mind, I simply remembered its funny face that would greet passersby, and I was able to go quickly and peacefully to sleep.

I had a client who described a fear he felt of being judged. When I asked him to draw a visual representation of his fear, he drew a dark cloud and explained that he felt as if he was surrounded by darkness.

When I asked him how he could turn it into something humorous, he looked at it for a moment and exclaimed, "Wait! That's my hair in the morning!"

He attached a head to the dark cloud, and suddenly it was nothing more than a ball of hair.

I asked if his hair could harm him, judge him, or keep him from progressing toward his goals, to which he responded, "Of course not!"

I invited him, from that day forward, any time he began to feel judged, to imagine the feeling was nothing more than his hair.

To my knowledge, that fear never bothered him again.

Once you establish your clients' root fear, invite them to draw a picture of it. Explain that it doesn't have to be a masterpiece, but simply some sort of visual representation of what they have been feeling.

Once finished, invite them to explain what they drew, and then verify, "When you see this image, do you feel fear?"

Once they say yes, invite your clients to then modify their drawing to something silly or humorous.

Only make suggestions if absolutely necessary; it is better for them to allow their own mind to come up with the new image.

Once they have, invite them to describe the new image to you. Again, it should be something that's funny or goofy.

Humor is the antidote of fear. It is difficult to laugh and feel fear at the same time.

Once your clients have described the new image to you, explain that this is all that fear ever was.

Ask, "Can (whatever their new image is) harm you?"

Once they respond that it cannot, encourage your clients to remember this new image any time they feel the old fear creeping in. Once they've done so enough times, the fear will eventually be completely eradicated.

4. Bigger Than the Fear

To perform this exercise, invite your clients to close their eyes and imagine their fear standing directly in front of them. Tell them to imagine that they have just swallowed a magic potion that causes them to grow indefinitely and their fear to shrink indefinitely.

Tell them to continue to see themselves growing bigger and bigger, stronger and stronger, more and more powerful, and to see their fear growing smaller and smaller, tinier and tinier, until they can easily smash it with their foot, pick it up in their hands and flick it away, or simply blow their fear into oblivion.

5. Ten Seconds of Courage

Have you ever heard the term "paralysis by analysis"?

This usually happens because a person believes they lack the courage to complete a certain task.

If you find this is the case with one of your clients, this tool may be for you.

After utilizing one or more of the tools in this chapter to help your clients overcome the root of their fear, remind them that they really only need to be courageous for ten seconds at a time.

If they feel impressed to reach out to someone, they only need to sum up ten seconds' worth of courage, or enough courage to simply dial someone's phone number or approach someone to begin a conversation.

Ten seconds doesn't seem like a long time, so this will usually alleviate the tension inside your clients' minds and get them out of the paralysis-by-analysis mode.

Invite them to repeat the words "Ten seconds of courage!" any time they need a boost of confidence to take the action required to reach a certain goal.

6. Boxes

There will come a time when you sense that some clients may be hiding something from you or withholding information regarding a limiting belief they need to eliminate. They may display closed-off body language by folding their arms or crossing their hands over their body. They might deflect probing questions you ask by sharing a completely unrelated story instead of answering the question itself.

When this happens, gently encourage your clients to actually answer the question. If you can tell there may still be something they are hiding, use this exercise.

Draw a number of boxes on a sheet of paper and explain that our subconscious minds are made up of several different compartments or "boxes." There is a box for money, a box for relationships, a box for spirituality, and so on. The purpose of mentoring is to explore the contents of each box and clean up or make adjustments when necessary.

Unfortunately, we sometimes have a box we like to sit on to resist exploring its contents.

Draw a person sitting on top of one of the boxes with their arms folded and an unhappy expression on their face. Explain that there can be times when we want to hide the contents of certain boxes from our mentors because we fear that opening and exploring these boxes will be painful, embarrassing, or shameful, but these are always the most important boxes to explore.

Gently ask them, "What is in the box you are sitting on?"

Your clients may get very quiet or emotional when you ask this question.

Give them a moment to compose themselves and process the question.

Send them love in your mind and reassure them that you are there to support them.

Ask permission to talk about whatever it is.

Show extreme kindness and acceptance. You will probably be diving into extremely personal issues.

Continue to ask your clients' permission before going any deeper into the breakthrough process.

If your clients say they don't know what is inside the box, simply say, "I know you don't know what's inside the box, but if you *did* know what was inside it, what would you say is there?" This is a simple tool to help a person get around the habit of saying the words "I don't know."

You may also invite them to use the Mirror Exercise (page 73 in *The Mentor's Toolbox*) to find out what is inside the box.

If your clients continue to resist and display stubborn energy, gently explain that you care about them.

Ask how serious they are about accomplishing their goals. If they say they are very serious, help them understand that whatever is in this box is keeping them from achieving their goals as quickly as they would like.

You are there to help.

Remind them that they are safe with you and that there will be no judgment.

If appropriate, remind them that you are not their religious leader, and that they do not have to give any details they do not wish to share, but that you would love to help them through whatever it is so they can move forward and progress more quickly.

Then kindly ask, "May we explore the contents of this box?"

When they are ready to talk about it, listen attentively to whatever they share. Use whatever additional tools you feel impressed to use to help them achieve a breakthrough.

7. The Wall

There will be times when your clients feel stuck.

They may say they have hit a wall with their progress.

Subconscious *walls* are interesting because they obstruct a person's view of their goals. If they can't visualize achieving their goals, they probably won't.

You will need to help your clients bring the wall down so they can "see" better.

When clients use this kind of language, give them a sheet of paper and invite them to draw a visual representation of the wall. Pay close attention to what they draw.

Once finished, ask them to identify what the wall is made out of in their mind.

Is it made of wood?

Concrete?

Bricks? (This is the most common answer.)

If your clients respond that the wall is made of bricks, invite them to draw the individual bricks in the wall.

Then ask them if all of the bricks represent several layers of the same limiting belief, if each *layer* of bricks represents a different limiting belief, or if each *individual* brick represents a separate limiting belief. Have them label what each brick, row of bricks, or the wall itself, represents. This may be fear, self-doubt, feelings of inadequacy, etc.

Doing so may seem daunting to them, especially if the wall is extremely tall. They probably haven't attempted to bring the wall down because of how daunting doing so appears to be.

This is where the fun begins.

If the wall is indeed made of bricks, explain that the only thing that needs to be removed from a brick wall to bring the entire wall down is the bottom layer of bricks.

The bottom layer supports the rest of the bricks, so if they are removed, the entire wall comes crashing down.

This often brings about a great sense of relief to the clients as they realize that removing their subconscious block isn't such a daunting task after all.

All you have to do now is address whatever the bricks at the bottom layer represent, utilizing one or more tools in your toolbox (e.g., the Fear-to-Funny Technique).

If your clients say the wall is made of stone, concrete, or anything that is completely solid, this usually means it represents one single, deeply rooted emotion or limiting belief.

Invite them to identify what it represents and then use the appropriate tool to help them bring the wall down once and for all.

8. Gingerbread Man Exercise

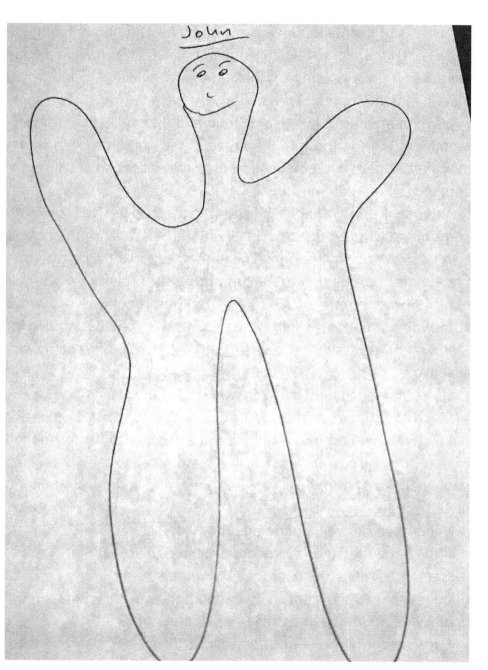

This is an excellent tool to use when your clients have resentment, hatred, or other negative emotions toward another person or group of people.

Invite your clients to draw a rough outline of a human being on a piece of paper. I am definitely not an artist, so whenever I do this exercise, it usually ends up looking like a lopsided gingerbread man; hence the name of the exercise.

Have them draw a face, some hair, and then label their "gingerbread man" at the top with the name of the person toward whom they harbor negative emotions. This will serve as a visual representation of that person.

Next, ask your clients to stand and prop up the drawing someplace where they can easily see it, such as on their chair or a desk. Then invite them to call the person's name out loud and ask for permission to fully express what has been on their mind. For example, if your clients feel resentment toward someone named Mary, they would draw a representation of Mary, stand up, and say *out loud*, "Mary, may I express myself to you?"

Have them wait until they hear a "Yes" in their mind.

Once they have, invite them to proceed to verbally express absolutely anything and everything that needs to be expressed to that person, holding nothing back, completely letting go, and continuing to speak until they feel their emotional tank is completely empty.

If they need to yell, encourage them to yell.

If they need to scream, encourage them to scream.

Remember, this must be done *out loud*.

If they try to do this only in their mind, the negative emotion will actually get lodged even deeper inside their bodies.

Expressing themselves out loud allows the energy to be released.

Once they feel they have verbally expressed everything they need to express, invite them to experience a *physical* release of emotion by destroying the paper.

If they feel they need to punch the paper, let them punch it.

If they want to rip its head off, let them rip its head off, or stomp on it, or tear it to shreds, or burn it—whatever it takes to allow a physical release of negative emotion to take place.

Once this is complete, invite your clients to pick up the pieces and prop them back up on the chair or wherever it was before.

Warn them that this next step may be the most difficult part of the exercise, because in order for full healing to take place, they must now ask for forgiveness for holding on to those negative emotions.

They might put up a fuss, saying, "But that person did this and this and this to me! Why should I ask for forgiveness from them?"

Gently remind your clients that they were the ones who held on to the negative emotions, and the words "Will you forgive me?" must leave their lips for this tool to be effective.

Invite them to look at what's left of the paper representation of the person and ask for forgiveness for holding on to the negative emotions toward them.

Finally, invite your clients to imagine the person's greatest and highest self standing in front of them, having heard everything that has been expressed, and then invite your clients to say the words they imagine that person's greatest and highest self would say to them. These may be words of apology, an expression of love, a deeper understanding, whatever it is; this is what completes the healing process.

Once they have completed this step, invite them to say, "I forgive you, and thank you for serving me," and then imagine themselves embracing.

9. Belief Breakthrough

(As taught by Kris Krohn and the founders of Limitless, shared with permission.)

Belief Breakthrough is designed to create awareness of any limiting beliefs that may be negatively impacting a person's results in life. The focus of this process is to exchange negative beliefs with positive beliefs in order to improve a person's happiness and results.

Guidelines for Belief Breakthrough

The following guidelines are important to consider when performing Belief Breakthrough:

Participants should be aware that the breakthrough processes often include exploring the inception of a negative belief. Volunteers may be invited to share the circumstances surrounding the creation of a limiting belief. Often the circumstances of a negative belief include a perceived traumatic event, whether real or imagined.

The title of "mentor" or "belief breakthrough coach" does not indicate a professional therapeutic license or degree. It designates someone who has been trained in and has demonstrated consistent ability to follow the scripts to replace negative, false, or limiting beliefs with positive and empowering beliefs.

Belief Breakthrough work is often cited for mending relationships, improving income, and even supporting participants in taking positive steps to improve their own health. Use of Belief Breakthrough is strictly for education, self-improvement, and life enhancement. No medical advice or claims are offered in any way. Neither I nor my company, Feel Well, Live Well, its facilitators and officers, offer any medical, therapeutic, diagnostic or curative treatments, and make no medical claims, whether for improving, treating, or curing any medical condition.

Feel Well, Live Well does not encourage public confession or disclosure of personal information that would normally only be discussed in a confidential setting, such as with a psychologist, psychiatrist, or religious leader.

Feel Well, Live Well advocates that the participant does not need to confront any individual to experience a breakthrough or overcome a challenge. Feel Well, Live Well teaches that problems lie within us and within our perceptions. Confronting another person is never required for an individual to alter their negative beliefs or improve their perceptions.

Confidentiality must be maintained for the protection and privacy of the participant. Unless the breakthrough coach has express permission from a participant, breakthrough sessions must remain confidential. For training or example purposes and in the proper setting, generalities of a session may be shared without disclosing personal details. We encourage breakthrough coaches to practice professional ethics.

Note: If you would like to experience Belief Breakthrough on a greater level, consider attending a Feel Well, Live Well live event or a live event hosted by Kris Krohn.

Belief Breakthrough Script

Step 1: Ground

"Do I have permission to facilitate this breakthrough? Great. I'm going to invite you to close your eyes and ground."

Use deep breathing with your eyes closed to get into a meditative state. The purpose of grounding is to disconnect from your thoughts and connect to your intuition. Clear your mind of all thoughts and prepare to receive answers.

Step 2: Identify a Limiting Belief

"What is the number-one limiting belief coming up for you?"

Listen for the intuitive answer. Trust that whatever comes up is exactly what you need to work on in this moment, especially if it doesn't seem to make sense.

Step 3: Explore Your Memories

"What is the first memory that comes up for you when you think this thought?"

Trust that whatever memory arises is the perfect place to focus your breakthrough work. If they hesitate, ask if they feel comfortable sharing the memory with you. You can still complete the process even if they don't vocalize the memory.

Step 4: Identify the Deeper Limiting Belief

"What did you decide about yourself when you experienced this?"

What comes from this step is deeper than the belief you found in Step 2 and is the one you really need to work with.

Step 5: Examine the Cost of the Limiting Belief

"Go ahead and open your eyes. What is the cost of believing this thought?"

Examine how this belief is showing up in your life. How has it affected your results in the past and present? How will it affect you in the future if you don't change it? Consider how it impacts other aspects of your life, including finances, physical health, relationships, and personal power.

Step 6: Give Yourself Permission to Shift

"Are you ready to replace this limiting belief with one that empowers you?"

Consciously choose to shift your beliefs and make a change.

Step 7: Create a New Belief

"Let's explore a new belief that will serve you better . . . "

Make the choice to change your old limiting belief to a new, empowering belief that will serve you better. State the new belief in first person and in the present tense.

Step 8: Rewrite Your Story

"I am going to invite you to close your eyes again and to go back to this memory. If you could invite anyone into this moment to show up for you and support you, who would that be? Great, let's invite them in. What is the first thing that happens as they step into this memory? What words are they sharing with you?"

Go back to the original memory from which you created your false belief. Imagine reinterpreting the experience in a way that serves you better and that is more aligned with the truth of the new belief. If necessary, in your imagination solicit the help of your higher self or someone who you deeply trust to support and assist you in rewriting your story. What words of support, encouragement, love, wisdom, and power would they offer to help you heal the pain of this experience and rewrite your story?

Step 9: Claim Your New Belief

"Repeat after me . . . (state the new belief). Let's find the best way for you to celebrate this choice. What are your next steps after making this new choice? Congratulations!"

Repeat the words of their new chosen belief. Shift the energy and emotion anchored to the memory to a strong positive emotion. Speak the words of their new belief they chose. State the new belief out loud with confidence, conviction, and power. Say it repeatedly. Declare it in the way that feels the most authentic to you. Invite them to commit to living this new belief and finding evidence to support it. Find a way to help them celebrate this new belief in the memory that came up or in their present life. A great way to end the breakthrough session is to ask for their next steps with the new choices they are now making.

10. Personal Belief Breakthrough (to use on yourself)

Step 1: Ground
Use deep breathing with your eyes closed to get into a meditative state. The purpose of grounding is to separate from your thoughts and connect to intuition. Clear your mind of all thoughts and prepare to receive answers.

Step 2: Identify a Limiting Belief
"What is the number-one limiting belief coming up for me?"

Listen for the intuitive answer. Trust that whatever comes up is exactly what you need to work on in this moment, especially if it doesn't seem to make sense.

Step 3: Explore Your Memories
"What is the first memory that comes up when I think this thought?"

Trust that whatever memory arises is the perfect place to focus your breakthrough work.

Step 4: Identify the Deeper Limiting Belief
"What did I decide about myself when I experienced this?"
What comes from this step is deeper than the belief you found in Step 2 and is the one you really need to work with.

Step 5: Examine the Cost of the Limiting Belief
"What is the cost of believing this thought?"

Examine how this belief is showing up in your life. How has it affected your results in the past and present? How will it affect you in the future if you don't change it? Consider how it impacts other aspects of your life, including finances, physical health, relationships, and personal power.

Step 6: Give Yourself Permission to Shift
Consciously choose to shift your beliefs and make a change.

Step 7: Create a New Belief
Make the choice to change your old limiting belief to a new, empowering belief that will serve you better. State the new belief in first person and in the present tense.

Step 8: Rewrite Your Story
Revisit the memory where you created your false belief. Imagine reinterpreting the experience in a way that serves you better and that is more aligned with the truth of the new belief. If necessary, solicit the help of your higher self or someone whom you deeply trust to support and assist you in rewriting your story. What words of support, encouragement, love, wisdom, and power would they offer to help you heal the pain of this experience and rewrite your story?

Step 9: Claim Your New Belief
Shift the energy and emotion anchored to the memory to a strong positive emotion. State your new belief out loud with confidence, conviction, and power. Say it repeatedly. Declare it in a way that feels most authentic to you. Commit to living this new belief, and find evidence to support it. Find a way to celebrate this

new belief in the memory that came up or in your present life. A great way to end the breakthrough is to determine your next steps with the new choices you are now making.

*Note: All of these mentoring tools (and many more) can be found in my book *The Mentor's Toolbox: 101 Powerful and Proven Tools for Reaching Higher Levels of Success*, which can be purchased on Amazon at this link: https://www.amazon.com/Mentors-Toolbox-Powerful-Reaching-Success/dp/0998786535/ref=mp_s_a_1_2?d-child=1&keywords=the+mentor's+tool+box&qid=1605648982&sr=8-2

This next exercise is for you to personally do in your persuasion journal:

Black Dot

●

Answer the following: What I see on this page is …

Do *not* proceed to the next page until you've answered this question in your persuasion journal.

Answers that have been shared from live Master of Persuasion audience members include:

- A single black dot
- A large chocolate cookie from a distance
- A black nose in a snowstorm
- Me in the center of future possibilities
- A dot that's not quite round

The interesting part of this exercise is most people choose to focus on the black dot on the page and completely ignore the white space that takes up the majority of the page.

Which one did you focus on?

Your answer may be an indication of what you tend to focus on in life. Is your glass half empty or half full? Do you focus on challenges or opportunities? Does life happen *to* you or *for* you?

What we focus on, expands.

Those that focus on health challenges tend to experience health challenges.

Those that focus on paying off debt tend to have a lot of debt to pay off.

Those that focus on negativity tend to attract negativity.

Those that focus on growth and abundance tend to have growth and abundance.

Those that focus on solutions tend to find solutions.

You get the idea.

Some people focus so much on the "black dots" in their life that they begin to *identify* with their black dots.

Have you ever heard someone justify some form of negative behavior by saying, "That's just who I am"?

Have you heard people say such phrases as,

"I am an addict."

"I am a smoker."

"I am diabetic."

"I am overweight."

"I am single."

… and the like?

Negative "I am" statements are among the most damaging of all statements because, whatever a person identifies with, their behavior must match it.

Consider that for a moment.

Someone who identifies as a smoker may go six months without a cigarette, but eventually they will return to smoking. Otherwise their subconscious mind thinks they are going crazy.

Someone who identifies with being overweight may lose several pounds of body fat, but eventually they will put the weight back on. Otherwise their subconscious mind thinks they are going crazy.

I once heard a story of a frog that is swimming around in a lake when a scorpion approaches him on the bank of the lake.

The scorpion says, "Mr. Frog, I need you to do me a favor. I need to get to the other side of the lake. Would you please give me a ride on your back?"

The frog responds, "Are you kidding me? No, absolutely not! You're a scorpion, I'm a frog. If I give you a ride, you'll sting me, and I'll die!"

The scorpion says, "Mr. Frog, you're not using your little frog brain. Think about that for a moment. If I sting you, yes, you'll die, but I'll die, too. We'll both be dead in the middle of the lake. Come on, I wouldn't do that."

The frog thinks, "He's got a point."

"All right," he tells the scorpion. "Hop on."

Halfway across the lake, the scorpion stings the frog.

With his last breath, the frog cries, "What did you do that for? You just killed me, but you're going to die, too! Why in the world would you do that?"

The scorpion responds, "Because I'm a scorpion, and that's what we scorpions do: we sting frogs."

Your behavior will match whatever you choose to identify with ...

... unless you choose a new identity.

Write the following in your persuasion journal:

I am *not* my black dot. I am a powerful child of the Divine who is destined for greatness. I am a master of persuasion!

Now place your hand over your heart and declare, "I am a master of persuasion!"

One of the first processes I do with my addiction recovery clients is help them separate their addictive behaviors from their identity.

"You may have struggled with addiction up to this point in your life, *but you are not an addict!*"

We help them replace their negative identities with positive identities, utilizing a number of mentoring tools, including creating an *identity board*.

Identity boards are a powerful way to reinforce the identity of the person you choose to become.

Consider the 5 Fs of Success:

- Faith
- Family
- Fitness
- Finances
- Fulfillment

What are two or three words that identify the kind of person you choose to become in each of these five areas?

Examples that some of my clients have used in each of the 5 Fs include:

Faith - Divine, Righteous, Disciple, Faithful, Apostle, Spiritual, Connected

Family - Loving Father, Loving Wife, Caring Parent, Tender, Orderly

Fitness - Strong, Powerful, Lean, Muscular, Fit, Ironman, Buff, Ripped

Finances - Free, Multibillionaire, Abundant, Generous, Excellent Steward

Fulfillment - World Traveler, Purpose, Joyful, Fulfilled, Peaceful

In your persuasion journal, write two to three words that match the identity you wish to create in each of the above five areas.

Next, find images that match the words you chose, print them, and cut them out.

Place these words and images on a poster board or directly on the wall above your bed. This is your identity board. Read them to yourself each day out loud, saying, "I am ..." before each word.

"I can see how powerful this tool is, Eric, but what if I have blind spots or black dots that are clouding my identity that I don't even realize are there?"

Most people have blind spots. This is why it is important to always have a skilled mentor who can help you recognize and overcome the blind spots and black dots in your life.

Find your mentors. Find people who have what you desire in life. Invest in working with them to help you create the life you desire. Olympic athletes never become Olympic athletes without the help of mentors. Billionaires don't become billionaires without mentors.

Write the following in your persuasion journal:

I overcome my blind spots and black dots by regularly investing in mentors.

Now place your hand over your heart and declare, "I am a master of persuasion!"

"Eric, even as I strive to implement the tools found in this book and improve who I am, will some people still choose to treat me unkindly, be disrespectful, or try to get me to make poor choices?"

Yes.

Sadly, there are some who choose to tear people down rather than build people up, who bully and manipulate others. It is important to learn to recognize and arm yourself against such tactics...

CHAPTER 9

ARMING YOURSELF

Have you noticed that certain people seem to be polarizing, no matter who the audience is?

It used to be that politics, romance, and religion were the only topics that were inappropriate to bring up at the dinner table. Now it seems that some people look for any excuse to choose to take offense.

More and more social media posts are emotionally charged rants against the latest political news or campaign.

In an age where more and more people can spew negativity while hiding behind their computer screens, emotions continue to rise, tempers continue to flare, and heated arguments are started over who is right and who is wrong.

Even so, masters of persuasion seek ways to stand up for what is right and make a difference in the lives of others. That's why it is important to learn to recognize tactics that seek to *destroy* and counter them with energy that seeks to *build*. We will be discussing several such tactics in this chapter.

Bullying

I was extremely chubby growing up. I was constantly bullied and ridiculed for my weight. It was not uncommon for me to come home from school, run into my room, slam the door shut, and burst into tears because of the mean things that were said about me.

According to Sherri Gordon, there are six forms of bullying:

Physical

This tends to be the most obvious and easiest to identify. Physical bullies are usually bigger, stronger, and more aggressive than those they bully. Hitting, kicking, slapping, and shoving are all examples.

Verbal

This includes teasing, name-calling, and demeaning others. Most of us have experienced this form of bullying at least once. It can leave deep emotional scars if not properly addressed.

Relational

This can be one of the most difficult to notice. It is when someone tries to sabotage the social standing of another to increase their own. They often gossip, spread rumors, lie, break confidences, and oust someone from social groups. It shows a major lack of confidence and self-esteem on the part of the bully.

This is typically found among middle-school kids and high schoolers wanting to fit in and be accepted by their classmates, but we find it quite a bit in the adult world as well. Coworkers will often gossip among themselves about other coworkers.

Even family members sometimes speak ill of one another.

People spread horrible things about businesses they don't like with the justification that they are simply "raising awareness," not realizing that, by talking about and adding energy to the problem, they are actually amplifying it. They feel justified in damaging a person's reputation merely because they chose to take offense at something that was said or done.

Cyberbullying

The most common form of cyberbullying is when someone posts something on social media that stirs the emotions of someone who has a different opinion. The latter then chooses to make comments that include name-calling, finger-pointing, and mean statements, such as, "It's people like you that are what's wrong with our society today!"

Another form of cyberbullying includes taking to social media to air one's grievances about another person, situation, or business. We call this "airing dirty laundry in public."

Sexual

Young women are often the target of sexual bullying, which may include crude comments about a girl's body or appearance, sexual name-calling, vulgar gestures, uninvited touching, or propositioning.

Prejudicial

Aimed at people of different races, religions, or sexual orientations. This type of bullying can include all five of the others. If noticed, it is best to report it immediately to proper authorities, such as teachers, administrators, or the police.

"So, Eric, what can be done when we see this happening? Are there tools we can use to protect ourselves and our loved ones from bullying?"

Yes!

If you or someone you know is experiencing bullying, even if the bully is your own mind, consider the following tools:

Change your beliefs about yourself.

Someone who regularly tolerates bullying may have a subconscious belief that they somehow deserve to be bullied.

Modifying how you view yourself can change how others view you.

Finding and replacing limiting beliefs about yourself can be a game changer. Use the process found on pages 118-120 to form new, more empowering beliefs about yourself.

Change how you view the bully.

Masters of persuasion understand that hurt people hurt people.

Bullies have a reason for taking out their pain on other people. This doesn't excuse or condone their behavior, but it does not serve you to hold on to negative emotions toward the bully. Doing so only serves the bully, because it gives power to them.

Bullies want you to feel hurt. Allowing yourself to change how you view the bully takes your power back.

Use the Gingerbread Man exercise found on pages 111-113 to release toxic emotions and view the bully in a new way.

Increase your confidence through fitness.

Increasing your fitness involves improving your physical, mental, and emotional health. It often requires finding healing for deeply rooted physical, mental, and emotional wounds. My own journey of releasing over eighty pounds involved letting go of long-lasting hurt that stemmed from my childhood and early adult years.

The more whole and complete you are, the more confident you become. The more confident you become, the less likely it is you will tolerate bullying.

If you would benefit from additional help and resources, email me at Eric@FeelWellLiveWell.com. I have a number of audio trainings and other resources to help you achieve permanent weight reduction, emotional and mental healing, and more. Email me with the subject "Help with Fitness" and let me know what kind of help you are looking for. I am happy to send you those resources for free as a special thank you for reading this book. Don't delay. Email me right away.

Body language

Bullies target those whom they view as weak and easy targets. If you were to watch for commonalities among victims of bullying, you would notice they often stand with most of their weight on one leg, meaning they are off balance. If pushed, they would easily fall over, sending a message that they are "pushovers."

A simple shift in their body language can make all the difference.

Standing with both legs firmly and evenly planted on the ground with their feet about shoulder length apart sends a message that they are strong, firm, and will not be taken advantage of.

Personal boundaries

A mentor once taught me the importance of having three rules, or boundaries, energetically planted in my mind. When others enter my personal space, they energetically pick up on my rules and are more inclined to follow them at a subconscious level.

My three rules are:

1. No dumping negativity
2. Be respectful
3. Be meticulous with your word

Write down three rules you desire everyone who interacts with you to follow in your persuasion journal.

Next, find images on the internet that represent each of your rules to lock them into the visual part of your brain. In your mind, imagine yourself taking a hammer and posting signs all over your energy field that have your three rules written on them.

Want to take this to the next level?

Grab an imaginary sign in the air and physically act out hammering your rules into the ground, making sound effects to go with it. Doing so helps it become real in your mind.

It is fascinating to watch people enter my energy field. On the rare occasion someone intends to say something negative to me, they will usually be huffing and puffing. Once they enter my personal space, they feel the energetic rules I've posted, and one of two things will happen: either they change course and walk away, or their demeanors change, they calm down, and we are able to have a productive discussion.

Redirecting the conversation

Bullies often try to establish dominance over others by making rude comments or asking rude questions. Knowing how to respond in a neutral but firm way can let the bully know you have self-respect and do not tolerate bullying.

Consider the following four ways to respond when someone makes a rude comment or asks you a rude question:

"That's interesting. Tell me more."

"That's interesting. Why would you say that to me?"

"That's interesting. Why would you do that?"

"That's interesting. Why would you ask me that?"

When using these responses, make sure to keep your countenance and tone of voice completely neutral. You are *not* trying to pick a fight. You are merely seeking to uncover their true intentions (it is entirely possible their intention was *not* to be disrespectful; it only seemed that way). Sometimes they aren't aware that what they said or did was unkind or disrespectful. These responses help them take a step back and ask themselves, "Well, why *did* I say/do/ask that?"

Report the issue to the right people.

If you become aware that someone is experiencing bullying, *never* tell them to simply ignore it. Doing so sends a message that you don't actually care about what is happening to them. Bullying can leave deep emotional and physical scars; telling someone to simply ignore it implies you aren't willing to help them come up with a lasting solution.

Genuinely listen to their concerns, validate what they are feeling, and reassure them that you will do all you can to help resolve the issue. If it is a child, this may include reporting the issue to a teacher at school or talking to the other child's parents. If it is an adult, show unconditional love and help them get the help they need.

Again, more than anything, help them feel loved and protected. They took a leap of faith in confiding in you. Please don't do anything to jeopardize that confidence.

Keep in mind that the people to inform about the bullying are the *right* people, meaning those who can actually do something to resolve the issue.

A mistake many people make is broadcasting their experiences publicly, often on social media, to thousands of people who are unable to do anything productive.

Doing so is counterproductive; those who see it on social media now have negative feelings toward the person and/or situation that serve no one.

This can also damage the reputation of those involved.

Some argue they are hoping to warn people away from the bully. Without all the facts and truly understanding the circumstances and the intentions of those involved, this often does much more damage than good. If, for example, the bully tries to turn his life around, there will be many who still carry negative feelings, thus making it much more difficult for full change to take place.

Masters of persuasion understand that it is often good to get involved if someone they love is experiencing bullying but only go to the proper authorities (i.e., school principal, the bully's parents, police, attorneys, etc.) who have the ability to make a difference in the situation.

Focus on the things you do want rather than what you don't want.

A movie came out not long ago that supposedly contained controversial material. Thousands of people took to social media to express their disgust and urge people not to go see it.

Can you guess what happened?

Millions of people went to see the movie who would never have heard about it had no one taken to social media to discuss it. Their rants served as advertising for the movie.

Whatever we focus on, expands.

Whatever we add energy to, grows.

Rather than adding energy to things they *don't* want, masters of persuasion focus on what they *do* want.

Mother Teresa famously said she would never attend an anti-war rally, but invite her to a pro-peace rally and she'd be there.

If you are against abortion, choose to put your energy toward parenthood, adoption, and the miracles of birth.

If you are against hate, choose to put your energy toward love.

Masters of persuasion choose *creation* energy rather than *destructive* energy.

This does *not* mean ignoring problems altogether. As previously discussed, if something needs to change, be an agent of change by going to the right people to make a difference, but avoid the temptation to add extra energy to issues you dislike.

Once you've reached out to the right people, focus your attention on issues you *do* like.

Choose forgiveness

Regardless of the challenges you have faced, it is important to forgive and rid yourself of toxic negative emotion.

Emotion is literally *energy in motion.*

Releasing this energy may actually attract fewer bullies into your life because *like attracts like*; if you hold onto negative emotion regarding bullying, you might continue to attract it until you've released it.

Keep in mind that forgiveness does *not* mean condoning the negative behavior, putting yourself in harm's way, or restoring the relationship to what it once was.

Forgiveness is not for the bully but for *you.*

Negative emotion is toxic to the body and can lead to various forms of dis-ease.

Forgiveness is nothing more than releasing toxic emotion from your body. Use the tools found in Chapter 8 to facilitate this process.

Gossip

A fun game I played as a kid was called Operator. Several people sit side by side, and the person at the far end would whisper something into the ear of the person next to them, who then whispers it in the ear of the next person, and so forth, down the line, until it gets to the very last person, who then stands up and shares what they heard. It's interesting to watch; usually the original message becomes skewed. By the time it reaches the last person, it is completely different.

How many times have you heard something from a family member, friend, coworker or neighbor about someone else? Perhaps something the other person said or did didn't sit well with them, and they felt the need to get revenge by dragging that person's name through the mud.

Gossip is any negative talk, either verbal or written, about another person who isn't present.

Whether it is true or false, gossip has long-lasting consequences.

Masters of persuasion *never* participate in gossip, especially passing it on.

If they happen to hear it, they respond, "That's interesting. What do you *like* about that person?" or, "That's interesting. I wonder if it's true. Let's call that person and find out what's really going on."

When others learn you do not tolerate gossip, they will be less inclined to pass it on.

It is OK to feel angry, annoyed, or frustrated at times, but it is *not* OK to vent or dump those emotions on another person. That is what journals are for. If you feel the need to express a dislike regarding something or someone, write it down. You may be surprised how great a relief that is.

If you feel like you still have more to say, go someplace where you can be totally alone and say what you wrote. Nature is a great place to do this. Again, make sure no one can hear you because, if they do, they will then have the negative energy inside them.

If someone offends you, be an adult and work it out in private *directly with that person.*

Gossiping about them will *not* solve anything; it only makes the gossiper look childish.

This principle is especially true in marriages.

Too many marriages fall apart because the couple has a disagreement, and one or both spouses call their friends or family members to vent about how mean the other spouse is.

Never speak ill of your spouse to another person. Only allow others to hear how wonderful your spouse is. When disagreements occur, go cool off, write down your frustrations, and then work it out with your spouse directly (and no one else).

"But, Eric, you don't know my spouse! They are never willing to work things out with me!"

You may be surprised how much of a difference releasing toxic emotion from within you can make. When you replace negative energy with positive energy, others often follow suit. The Gingerbread Man Exercise on page 111 is a great place to start.

Instead of learning about other people and businesses from previous acquaintances or clients, masters of persuasion go straight to the source to form their own opinions.

This concept also holds true with businesses.

You wouldn't go to McDonald's to learn about Burger King, nor would you go to Walmart to learn about Costco. If you want to find out what a business is truly like, find out for yourself. Masters of persuasion are mature enough to form their own opinions rather than simply believing what other people say.

Refrain from gossip, be mature enough to form your own opinions, and speak only kind words about others, especially your spouse.

Recognizing Manipulation Tactics

As discussed in Chapter 2, manipulation is influencing someone into a win-lose situation. There are several tactics that those who practice manipulation, whether consciously or accidentally, might use, as listed below (which includes information from authors George K. Simon, Jeremy Goff, and Brad Wilcox).

Please note that I believe most people are inherently good and are trying the very best they can in life. Many of these tactics are probably used without people realizing it. I only bring these up so you can recognize them when others use them and ensure you only use *persuasion,* never manipulation.

Warning: This section may be extremely triggering. It may be tempting to stop reading this book before you finish this chapter. Hang in there. A major breakthrough may occur within a few short pages.

Bullying: As discussed previously, there are several forms of bullying, which usually involve exercising some sort of dominion over someone by force or coercion.

Lying by commission: Presenting false information as truth. (For example, "Did you take the trash out?" "Of course I did!")

Lying by omission: Withholding a significant amount of truth. (For example, "Why did you leave your previous employment?" "It wasn't a good environment for me to be in." "Were you fired?" "......")

Half-truths: It is not uncommon for some people to tell a number of truths to gain one's confidence to then fit in one lie. (For example, "I've been on the keto diet for a year now, and I haven't lost an ounce!" The statement that they've been on the keto diet for a year is true, and so is the fact they haven't lost an ounce because, in reality, they have lost twenty pounds.)

Irrelevant appeals: Saying something that is true but completely irrelevant to the topic at hand, done to detract from truth. (For example, "I believe something needs to be done about gun control." "I can't stand tater tots!")

Personal attack: Attempting to destroy someone's character instead of addressing the issue they present. (For example, "I believe something needs to be done about global warming." "You're a fraud!")

Appeals to the stone: Blatantly dismissing someone's opinion, argument, or statement without providing a reason for its dismissal. (For example, "Something needs to be done about immigration." "That's nonsense!")

Appeals to authority: Citing a ridiculous opinion of someone who happens to be in a position of authority. (For example, "Consuming less refined sugar can help decrease obesity." "That's not true! I know a medical doctor who says consuming large amounts of refined sugar has zero effect on our bodies!")

False dilemma: Thinking there are only two options in a given situation. Because they would do something a certain way, they believe someone who doesn't do things that same way must not exist or care about people, etc. (For example, "If you *really* cared about people, you wouldn't charge for your services.") This is especially dangerous for those who genuinely care about people and value their own integrity. It can lead victims to giving in because they don't like having their integrity questioned.

Unfair comparisons: Similar in feel to false dilemmas, this is blatantly comparing two unlike things, "apples to oranges." (For example, "My church only asks me to pay 10% in tithing. Why do restaurant servers want me to tip 20%?")

Hasty generalizations: Taking the experience from one or a few and generalizing it for all. (For example, "I met an attorney once, and he was a jerk. Therefore, *all* attorneys must be jerks!")

Hearsay: Presenting rumors and information received from other people that cannot be substantiated as truth. (For example, "I've been told that person is racist!")

Out of context: Saying something that is true while purposely withholding the surrounding words or circumstances to twist the truth. (For example, "He took the lives of more than a dozen people!" ... without mentioning that he fought in World War II.)

Mudslinging: Use of insults and accusations, especially unjust ones, with the aim of damaging the reputation of an opponent. (For example, "Don't vote for this politician; he's an idiot and unfit to lead!")

Exaggerations: Representing something as better or worse than it really is. (For example, "When the economy tanked in 2008, 90% of Americans were out of work.")

Denial: Refusing to admit to wrongdoing. (For example, "Son, your teacher caught you cheating on your exam. What happened?" "I would *never* do such a thing! My teacher just hates me!")

Deflection: Attempting to shift focus off something that is their responsibility by pointing out someone else's mistakes or flaws. (For example, "Robert, you promised to hand in your report by yesterday at noon, and I still don't have it." "*You* promised to give me a raise, and you didn't.")

Rationalization: Excuses made for inappropriate behavior. (For example, "Sweetie, your teacher tells me you punched another girl in class. Why would you do such a thing?" "She deserved it! She is mean to everyone!")

Minimization: This is a type of denial coupled with rationalization. The person practicing manipulation asserts that their behavior is not as harmful or irresponsible as someone else was suggesting; for example, saying that a taunt or insult was only a joke.

Selective attention/inattention: Refusing to pay attention to anything that may distract from their agenda. (For example, "I don't want to hear it.")

Diversion: Not giving a straight answer to a straight question and, instead, being diversionary, steering the conversation onto another topic. (For example, "Jim, did you take Sally's lunch?" "You know, it's interesting you would say that, because I had lunch at this amazing restaurant last week ...")

Evasion: Similar to diversion but giving irrelevant, rambling, vague responses. (For example, "Bradley, did you hit your brother?" "I … uh … well … you see …")

Covert intimidation: Throwing the victim onto the defensive by using veiled, subtle, indirect or implied threats.

Guilt trip: Suggesting to a conscientious victim that they do not care enough, are too selfish, have it easy, and the like. This usually results in the victim feeling bad, keeping them in a self-doubting, anxious, and submissive position. Because this isn't actual "guilt," it would be more accurately called a "shame trip."

Shaming: Using sarcasm and put-downs to increase fear and self-doubt in the victim. Some use this tactic to make others feel unworthy and, therefore, defer to them. Shaming tactics can be very subtle, such as a fierce look or glance, an unpleasant tone of voice, rhetorical comments, or subtle sarcasm. It is a way to foster a sense of inadequacy in the victim.

Vilification: More than any other, this tactic is a means of putting the victim on the defensive while simultaneously masking the aggressive, manipulative intent. It often involves falsely accusing the victim of being an abuser or manipulator in response to the victims standing up for or defending themselves or their position. Ironically, accusing someone of manipulation when their actions are not so is, in and of itself, a form of manipulation and falls under this category.

Playing the victim role: Portraying oneself as a victim of circumstance or of someone else's behavior in order to gain pity, sympathy, or evoke compassion, and thereby get something from another. Caring and conscientious people cannot stand to see anyone suffering, making it easy to play on sympathy to get cooperation.

Playing the servant role: Cloaking a self-serving agenda in the guise of a service to a more noble cause; for example, saying they are acting in a certain way to be "obedient" to or in "service" to an authority figure or "just doing their job."

Seduction: Using charm, praise, flattery, or overtly supporting others in order to get them to lower their defenses and give their trust and loyalty. Seducers may also offer help with the intent of gaining trust and access to an unsuspecting victim they have charmed.

Projecting the blame (blaming others): Projecting one's own thinking onto the victim, making the victim look like they have done something wrong. This involves claiming the victim is the one who is at fault for believing lies they were conned into believing, as if the victim forced the person practicing manipulation to be deceitful. All blame is done in order to make the victim feel shameful about making healthy choices, correct thinking, and positive behaviors. It is frequently used as a means of psychological and emotional manipulation and control. Manipulators lie about lying, only to remanipulate the original, less believable story into a "more acceptable" truth that the victim will believe. Projecting lies as truth is another common method of control and manipulation. They may falsely accuse the victim as "deserving to be treated that way," often claiming the victim is crazy and/or abusive.

Feigning innocence: Suggesting that any harm done was unintentional or that they did not do something they were accused of. They may put on a look of surprise or indignation. This tactic makes the victim question their own judgment and/or sanity.

Feigning confusion: Playing dumb by pretending not to know what the victim is talking about or pretending to be confused about an important issue brought to their attention. It usually involves intentionally confusing the victim in order for the victim to doubt their own accuracy of perception. Some may even use cohorts to help back up their story.

Brandishing anger: Using anger to brandish sufficient emotional intensity to shock the victim into submission. This is usually only an act. They want what they want and get "angry" when denied. Brandishing anger is often used as a manipulation tactic to avoid confrontation, avoid telling the truth, or to further hide intent. It may even involve going to the police or falsely reporting abuses that are intentionally contrived to scare or intimidate the victim into submission. Blackmail and other threats of exposure are other forms of brandishing anger and manipulation, especially when the victim refuses initial requests or suggestions. Anger can also be used to avoid telling truths at inconvenient times or circumstances, or as a tool to ward off inquiries or suspicion. The victim becomes more focused on the anger than the manipulation tactic.

Appeals to experience: Using one's age or experience to prove he or she is "right." (For example, "Jim, I don't believe you're doing that correctly." "Of course I am! I've been doing this a lot longer than you have! I know what I'm doing!")

Sarcasm: Using irony to mock or convey contempt. (For example, "John, will you be attending my party this weekend?" "Hmm … let's see … spend time with my hot girlfriend or go to your lame party? I just *can't* seem to determine which one I would rather do …")

Appeals to the masses: When someone tries to manipulate how someone else feels and fails, they will often try to manipulate how their victim is seen by others. This may include public posts on social media to "vent" about their victim, writing negative reviews about businesses that didn't cater to unrealistic demands, or inviting friends or family members to "back them up." ("Hey, Debbie! You look really fat today!" "No, I actually look quite beautiful because I *am* beautiful. Thanks, though!" "Hey, everyone, look at Debbie! Doesn't she look fat!?!")

Justification by claiming the lesser of two evils: Similar to minimization, this involves deflection away from taking responsibility for a wrongdoing or lack of integrity by stating that what they did wasn't as bad as what they could have done or what others might have done. ("Yes, I no-showed my appointment, but at least I didn't lie and make up some lame excuse about it!")

Unsolicited criticism: Offering feedback or criticism to someone outside one's stewardship or without permission. Masters of persuasion always ask for permission before offering feedback or constructive criticism.

I recognize that this can be an extremely heavy topic. Many have used similar tactics, either knowingly or unknowingly. Again, my purpose in including this extensive list is to help you be aware of them in your own life so that appropriate changes can be made.

Write the following four sentences in your persuasion journal, leaving enough space in between each one for journaling:

I have (either knowingly or unknowingly) used the following tactics ...

A better way of doing things would be ...

I now 100% commit to changing ...

This will have a positive impact in my life in the following ways ...

Be completely honest with yourself.

What kind of difference would it make in your life if you replaced all manipulation tactics with persuasion tactics and took a stand for good?

If you find yourself using any one or more of the above-mentioned tactics, stop immediately. Nothing good ever comes from manipulation.

"Eric, I feel like I have to walk on eggshells now to avoid using any kind of manipulation tactics!"

It may seem like that at first. Don't worry; no one is perfect. Simply do your best to replace any form of manipulation with persuasion and forgive yourself and others when accidental mistakes happen.

"Eric, I feel extremely triggered! I have been a victim of manipulation my entire life! What can I do?"

Most people will experience some form of manipulation at different times during their lives. The key is the ability to recognize manipulation when it happens, having firm personal boundaries, realizing that most people are honestly doing the very best they can with the resources they currently have, and allowing yourself to forgive quickly.

The following is a powerful forgiveness exercise I invite you to do right now. Please go someplace where you won't be overheard or disturbed.

Take several deep breaths in through your nose and blow them out through your mouth. Clear your mind and allow yourself to be fully present.

Imagine that everyone who has ever used any form of bullying or manipulation against you, either knowingly or accidentally, is standing before you.

Say, "May I fully express myself to all of you?"

Wait until you hear a "Yes" in your mind.

Once you do, say very clearly (out loud; do *not* do this exercise only in your mind. It *must* be vocalized), "You are all here because you have used bullying or manipulation tactics against me at some point. I need you all to know that I will no longer tolerate any such behavior. I am not someone who will be bullied or manipulated. I am a powerful, divine creator and master of persuasion. Thank you for helping me learn the lessons I needed to learn. Those of you willing to treat me with only the highest levels of respect and integrity from now on may stay in my life. The rest of you must go. I now release you to live your lives in light and love. I forgive you for all that has been done. You have no power over me. I release you now. Just go!"

As you say the last two words, bring your hand to your mouth as if you were holding everyone in your palm and blow, as if you were blowing them all away.

Next, imagine that everyone *you* have ever bullied or manipulated in any way, either knowingly or accidentally, is standing before you.

Say, "May I fully express myself to all of you?"

Wait until you hear a "Yes" in your mind.

Once you do, say (out loud), "My dearest friends, thank you for coming into my life at the appropriate times. I have used manipulation tactics against you, and that is *not* OK! I humbly apologize now and give you my word that I will *never* do so again. Will you all please forgive me?"

Imagine all of them nodding their heads.

If more people come to your mind that you need to forgive or ask forgiveness from, repeat the process.

If you or someone you know is experiencing bullying, manipulation of any kind, or anything of the sort, seek immediate help. Such abuse can do very real physical, mental, emotional, and spiritual damage. Email my team at Office@FeelWellLiveWell.com with the subject "Please help" right away. We can put you in touch with licensed professionals who can help you find the resources to achieve the healing you need (often at no charge). Don't delay. Seek help right away.

Take a moment and write a firm commitment to yourself and others in your persuasion journal regarding how you will utilize the tools you learned in this book for good. Begin as follows:

I _____ (insert your name) now 100% commit to implementing the tools, skills, and strategies found in this book by ...

This will make a difference in the lives of others because ...

This will make a difference in my own life because ...

Once you do this exercise, email me your responses. I want to hear from you. Send an email to Eric@FeelWellLiveWell.com with the subject "Master of Persuasion book." Tell me your name, where you are from, and your answers to the above-mentioned journal prompts. Once you do, I will have a gift for you to help you make an even bigger difference in the lives of others.

You are powerful.

You make a difference in the lives of others.

You have the ability to create the life of your dreams for yourself and your family.

You are a master of persuasion!

Now place your hand over your heart and declare, "I am a master of persuasion!"

My Gift to You

I want to personally thank you for purchasing and reading my book. I hope you have found it useful and will continue to use the tools found within its pages to change your own life and the lives of those whom you influence.

Because you read this book, I want to offer you a special "thank you" gift worth nearly $4,000.00. In order to get the most out of this book, I am offering you two tickets to our next three-day Master of Persuasion event, live in Salt Lake City, Utah, so you and a guest may take the skills you learned in this book to a new level. (More information about this seminar, including when the next one will be held, can be found at https://www.feelwelllivewell.com/master-of-persuasion/.) Tickets are usually $1,995.00 each, but if you will commit to being there for the entire three days and playing full-on as if you had paid full price, you and a guest may register for the next class at *no* charge. To claim your free tickets, email ClientServices@FeelWellLiveWell.com and let my team know you have read this book and would like to attend our upcoming Master of Persuasion event. Include your name and a phone number to reach you, and someone will be in touch to help you claim your free tickets.

You are meant to be a master of persuasion. Join us at our next event, and become the person you were meant to be. We'll see you there!

Acknowledgments

A major thank you to Heather Bailey, Jack Canfield, T. Harv Eker, Tad James, Garrett Gunderson, Ron Williams, Dr. M. T. Morter Jr., Tom Schreiter, Brendon Burchard, Tony Robbins, Kris Krohn, Sharon Lechter, Napoleon Hill, Ann Webb, Gary Chapman, Dr. Hartman, Noah St. John, and many more for the inspiration and creation of many of the tools found in this book, and the effect you have had in my life. You truly are pioneers in the industry and are changing lives all over the world.

About the Author

Eric Bailey is a professional mentor, trainer, and advanced holistic healthcare practitioner. Over the years, he has closely observed the habits of highly successful people. Implementing what he has learned, he has seen massive growth in his healthcare practice, health, and relationships, especially with his beautiful wife, Heather, and five beautiful children. In one year alone, he grew his monthly income more than a hundredfold, going from welfare to wealthy and becoming a millionaire by age 30. He went on to go from the verge of divorce, entrenched in addictive behavior, obese, and deeply depressed, to a red-hot marriage, totally free, releasing more than eighty pounds, and absolutely loving life.

He now seeks to share his secrets to success, which absolutely anyone can use. Eric is a powerful motivational speaker and has impacted the lives of hundreds of thousands of people around the world through his books, audio trainings, YouTube channel (Feel Well, Live Well), live seminars, personal mentoring programs, and healthcare practice throughout Utah.

His greatest desire is to improve the lives of millions of people around the globe by helping them achieve vibrant health, massive wealth, and successful, loving relationships.

Master of Persuasion

60039477R00095